Shall I be accused [...] much? But it will [...] always been attacked.... And lastly, what of my ambition? Oh, no doubt, such is there to be found, and in good supply. But the greatest and loftiest that ever was!

I have always thought that sovereignty resided in the people. In fact, the imperial government was a kind of republic....

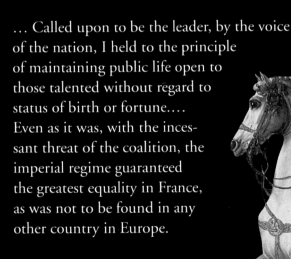

… Called upon to be the leader, by the voice
of the nation, I held to the principle
of maintaining public life open to
those talented without regard to
status of birth or fortune….
Even as it was, with the inces-
sant threat of the coalition, the
imperial regime guaranteed
the greatest equality in France,
as was not to be found in any
other country in Europe.

My rise is without antecedent, for it was accompanied by no crime. I have delivered fifty orderly battles …

… almost all of which I have won. I have devised and put into force a legal code that will have my name living on in the most distant posterity. From nothing, I raised myself to the ranks of the most powerful monarch in the world. Europe was at my feet. My ambition was great, I confess, but brought about by events and the opinion of the great masses.

Consolidation of forces, action and
resolve to perish in glory.
These are the three principles
of the art of war ...

… that have always brought me
good fortune in all my operations.
Death is nothing;
but to live defeated
and without glory is
to die every day…. Glory
exists only where there is danger….
Peace is a word devoid of meaning;
it is a glorious peace that we need.

I am so identified with our marvelous achievements, our monuments, our institutions, all of our national acts that one cannot sever me from them without causing affront to France....

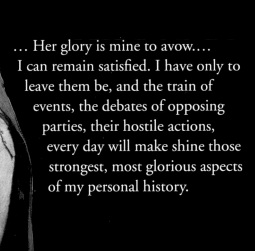

… Her glory is mine to avow.… I can remain satisfied. I have only to leave them be, and the train of events, the debates of opposing parties, their hostile actions, every day will make shine those strongest, most glorious aspects of my personal history.

CONTENTS

1 SON OF THE REVOLUTION
13

2 THE CONQUEST OF POWER
33

3 THE FOUNDER OF CONTEMPORARY FRANCE
53

4 THE GOD OF WAR
71

5 THE FALL
101

DOCUMENTS
129

Chronology
150

Filmography
152

Further Reading
153

List of Illustrations
153

Index
156

Credits
159

NAPOLÉON
"MY AMBITION WAS GREAT"

Thierry Lentz

DISCOVERIES®
HARRY N. ABRAMS, INC., PUBLISHERS

For a long time Napoléon Bonaparte's heart wavered between Corsica and France. Then this child of the Enlightenment was seized by the Revolution. He would owe everything, from early experiences in the exercise of power to military victories, to the great upheaval that disrupted France beginning in 1789.

CHAPTER ONE
SON OF THE REVOLUTION
(1769–99)

To understand Napoléon, one must consider the circumstances of his accession. Without the Revolution, he would have done nothing and would have been nothing. He owed everything to it, and he returned to it all that it had given him. Though he brought it to an end, he never betrayed it. One cannot understand Napoléon by dehumanizing him: He was a man. Ambitious, tyrannical, kind, and generous, all at the same time. Right: Bonaparte as a child; left: the young general at the Bridge of Arcole.

"What memories Corsica has left me with! I rejoice at her settings, her mountains."

Napoleone Buonaparte was born on August 15, 1769, in Ajaccio, Corsica, which had been French for only one year, following a treaty between Louis XV and the Republic of Genoa. He was the second son of one of the island's prominent families. His father, the lawyer Carlo Buonaparte (1746–1785), had fought beside Pasquale Paoli for the independence of Corsica for a long time before joining ranks with the French occupation. His mother, the beautiful Maria Letizia Ramolino (1750–1836), bore twelve children in succession.

Carlo Buonaparte did everything possible to gain entry into French polite society. Thanks to the patronage of Corsica's powerful French governor, Louis-Charles-René de Marbeuf (who, despite a persistent rumor to the contrary, was not the father of the future emperor), he was able to enter into the minor nobility. Consequently his two eldest sons, Joseph and Napoléon, were admitted to schools reserved for the disenfranchised nobility.

In 1778 Napoléon enrolled in the secondary school in Autun; in 1779 he entered the military college in Brienne; and in 1784 he joined the military academy in Paris, where he obtained the rank of second lieutenant in the artillery. His career was established: He would be an officer. On November 3, 1785, he took up his first posting with the La Fère regiment stationed in Valence.

"Oh, Rousseau!… In the interest of virtue, you should have been immortal!"

The young lieutenant was not particularly enamored of garrison life or military maneuvers. Melancholic and solitary, he preferred reading and studying. He was a child of the

Carlo Buonaparte (left), lawyer to the superior counsel of Corsica and deputy to the nobility of the island, died prematurely in 1785 from a cancer of the stomach, also the cause of Napoléon's death. (Below: extract from the certificate of nobility presented to Napoleone de Buonaparte in 1779.) His marriage to Maria Letizia Ramolino

Certifions au Roi que Napoleone de Buonaparte né le 15 d'Août mil sept cent soixante-neuf, fils de Noble Charles-Marie de Buonaparte Député de la Noblesse de Corse et de Dame Marie-Letitia Romolino sa femme, …

Enlightenment—the intellectual movement based on reason, tolerance, and the questioning of authority—and his desire was to be a man of letters. He sought his future in the ideas of the philosopher Jean-Jacques Rousseau, who argued for equality and against absolute monarchy and religious orthodoxy.

Corsica's fight for independence, first from Genoa, then from France, caused its native son's allegiance to waver. He would find himself—an officer commissioned by Louis XVI—helping first to promote Corsican nationalism and then, just a few years later, to suppress a Corsican revolt against the French occupation. All the while he was inspired by the ideals fueling the French Revolution (1789–99), when France deposed its king and struggled to reshape its government.

Napoléon's military superiors granted him many furloughs to attend to family matters after the death of his father. He was absent from his regiment from September 1786 to September 1787, from January to June 1788, from September 1789 to February 1791, from September 1791 to

(above) produced twelve children. Eight of them would reach adulthood: Joseph (born in 1768), Napoléon (1769), Lucien (1775), Elisa (1777), Louis (1778), Pauline (1780), Caroline (1782), and Jérôme (1784). One would become emperor; four, kings; and one, queen.

May 1792, and from October 1792 to June 1793. The Royal Army and then (after the overthrow of the monarchy in 1792) the Republican Army apparently did not limit the young officer's leaves.

It was in Corsica, based in Ajaccio and Bastia, that he most actively partook in the beginnings of the French Revolution. Paoli, named the island's military governor in 1790, received him icily but assigned him a few missions; on February 22, 1793, in the ranks of a volunteer Corsican battalion fighting in Sardinia, he experienced his baptism of fire.

Following each leave Napoléon returned to service in his original regiment. In July 1792 he was promoted to captain. Although outraged by the Parisian mob storming the Tuileries Palace on August 10, 1792, his attachment to the Revolution was undiminished. France was leading the world toward Liberty. To fight for France was to fight for Corsican liberty.

Paoli's strategy was different. He believed the island had to be independent from France—at any cost. In April 1792 he began drawing closer to England, France's longtime enemy. A parting of

Vindictive toward the Buonapartes, Pasquale Paoli pushed Napoléon, by his prejudice and political choices, into the arms of the French. Below: the final meeting of Napoléon, to the left, and Paoli, center.

ways with the young officer was inevitable. In June 1793 Paoli, supported by the English army, expelled the French; Bonaparte's family fled to Toulon, in southeastern France. By circumstance and adherence to the ideals of the Revolution, Bonaparte chose France. He and his family adopted the French spelling of their name in 1796.

"I do not know how one could deny the talent of Robespierre. He was far superior to those around him."

"Napoléon's reputation began at the siege of Toulon" (left), as the emperor would write about himself. "Everyone who had witnessed his actions predicted the career that he then fulfilled." Bonaparte was satisfied with a conservative use of artillery—something that was terribly overused by the revolutionary armies, where ability was cruelly lacking. Such political strategies would lead to his rapid promotion. At this point, Bonaparte was already referred to as "the most civil of generals." Below: Bonaparte as a young general.

Bonaparte a Jacobin? Everything about his demeanor seemed so. He certainly admired Maximilien Robespierre, a leader of the Jacobin Club of radical revolutionaries. Bonaparte's writings during the time, such as the famous *Supper at Beaucaire* (1793), were those of an ardent republican, an enemy of the federalists. His friendships with Augustin Robespierre (Maximilien's brother) and Louis-Marie-Stanislas Fréron, a revolutionary politician, as well as the circumstances of his flight from Corsica, all define him as a partisan of the revolutionary government, which consolidated its power during the repressive Reign of Terror (1793–94).

As artillery commander of the army that laid siege in September 1793 to Toulon, then in the hands of the English, he suggested the maneuver adopted by the military to retake the city and participated in the operation. Toulon was liberated on December 19, 1793, and Bonaparte was promoted to brigadier general on December 22. In Paris Robespierre had other ideas for the future career of Augustin's friend. Had Robespierre bestowed upon him

the command of the Paris National Guard, Bonaparte would without a doubt have accompanied him to the scaffold.

On 9 Thermidor Year II (July 27, 1794, by the Revolutionary calendar the Jacobins instituted in 1793) Robespierre and his allies were overthrown; they were executed the following day. On August 9 Bonaparte was arrested and imprisoned in Nice. He was freed August 20, thanks to the efforts of relatives who had escaped the purges that followed the coup. As France sought a new form of government Bonaparte sided first with the Thermidor National Convention and then with the Directory, the new regime under the leadership of Director Paul Barras. (The Directory would give way in 1799 to the Consulate, which would give way to the Empire in 1804.)

"From the time of the Directory, I was truly in Barras's heart."

Bonaparte was ordered to join the Army of the West but declined to take up his posting. Legend has it that he refused because he did not want to make war with

Before disbanding, the Convention decided that two-thirds of its members would hold seats in the chambers of the Directory, thus preserving a "revolutionary" majority. The royalists, thinking they would carry along the moderates, attempted a coup on 13 Vendémiaire Year IV (October 5, 1795). Following the orders of Director Barras (left), the army quelled the riots. Bonaparte, an artilleryman, forcibly drove back the threatening mass descending upon the Tuileries, the site of the assembly. Above: Bonaparte in front of Saint Roch Church.

other Frenchmen—the *chouans,* counterrevolutionaries in the Vendée. Another explanation is that he preferred a command in Provence, closer to his lover at the time. Barras assigned him to the topographical office at the Ministry of War in Paris, where he impressed his comrades. Nevertheless, in early September 1795 the government ordered him to take up his post with the Army of the West. Bonaparte refused and was struck from the list of employed generals.

The turmoil engulfing the government when its new constitution came into force presented him with an opportunity to reestablish himself. Summoned by Barras on 13 Vendémiaire Year IV (October 5, 1795) to help defend the Republic against royalist rioters, he bombarded a group of insurgents on the steps of Saint Roch Church in Paris. At a tribune of the National Convention, Fréron insisted that the Assembly remember the one who had done so much to save them.

Bonaparte's future was set. On October 16, 1795, he was appointed major general and then, some ten days later, commander of the Army of the Interior.

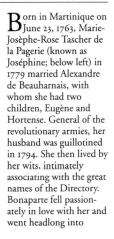

Born in Martinique on June 23, 1763, Marie-Josèphe-Rose Tascher de la Pagerie (known as Joséphine; below left) in 1779 married Alexandre de Beauharnais, with whom she had two children, Eugène and Hortense. General of the revolutionary armies, her husband was guillotined in 1794. She then lived by her wits, intimately associating with the great names of the Directory. Bonaparte fell passionately in love with her and went headlong into

Barras facilitated not only Bonaparte's military career but also his private life, passing on to Napoléon his own "incomparable friend," Joséphine de Beauharnais, the widow of a general guillotined

marriage. They wed on March 9, 1796. He would forgive her everything, from her vast spending to her marital infidelities. Above: an engraving depicting their engagement and the couple's signatures from the marriage certificate.

during the Reign of Terror. The wedding took place on March 9, 1796; their honeymoon was cut short, however, as Bonaparte had been appointed head of the Army of Italy on March 2 and ordered to take up his post two days after his marriage.

"Already I sensed the world flee from beneath me, as if I were being swept up into the skies."

France was struggling externally as well as internally. Eager to export its revolutionary ideals and expand its domain, the country between 1792 and 1802 would be continually at war with European monarchies aghast at the 1793 executions of Louis XVI and Marie Antoinette. The Italian campaign began in April 1796. In a succession of victories the French forced the Austrians to retreat, taking Montenotte, Millesimo, Mondovi, Lodi, and Milan. Austria's summer offensive, France's strategic withdrawal and counteroffensive, and the victory at Castiglione on August 5, 1796, enabled Bonaparte to reclaim lost ground. He was using his soldiers' legs to win the war. Some of his divisions covered six to ten miles more each day than their adversaries. The Austrian army could only hope that its far greater number of troops would prevail.

By the end of autumn, however, that had not happened. Just as he had during the summer, Bonaparte retreated. Then Bonaparte led his troops in an assault on the Austrian forces in Arcole, a small village in northern Italy; the Battle of the Bridge of Arcole raged from November 15 to 17. This defeat of the Austrians led to the Battle of Rivoli (January 14, 1797), the most stunning victory of the campaign. The French conquest of the Po Valley opened the route to Vienna. Austria sought a cease-fire and on April 18 signed the preliminaries of a peace treaty in Leoben.

Installed at his headquarters in Mombello, Bonaparte transformed himself into a proconsul. He developed a system of "political exploitation of the victory" (Jean Tulard). His endeavors expanded to other initiatives, such as the *Journal of Bonaparte and Virtuous Men* that appeared for a time in Paris. Little by little the name "Bonaparte" permeated the salons there. He was the man

After the Battle of Arcole, Bonaparte risked being caught in a pincer by two corps of the Austrian army. He fought the stronger of the two at Rivoli (below). The first Italian campaign (right: a map of the French and Austrian offenses) came to an end with Austria's (temporary) surrender, a dramatic confirmation of Napoléon's military and political gifts.

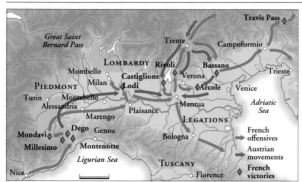

In Italy Bonaparte built up from among his officers his base of the loyal and the obliged. Thus did Berthier, Lannes, Sérurier, Augereau, Murat, Lasalle, and Masséna, among others, enter the annals of history with him. In Paris prominent politicians like Talleyrand began to think "there is a future there," despite the flaws in the Treaty of Campoformio Bonaparte negotiated in 1797.

of the hour, the general who had conquered and was governing Italy.

With his creation of sister republics, organization of civil administration, requisitions, confiscations, levying of taxes, invasion of Venice, and even, when necessary, repression of democrats on the

The Battle of Arcole, November 15–17, 1796

On the first day of the battle, Bonaparte, with flag in hand, attempted to lead his men across the bridge over the Alpone River. The attempt was brief. Pushed back, the general-in-command fell into the marsh and nearly drowned. After the eventual victory, he embellished his tales of the Bridge of Arcole. Dozens of popular engravings depicted him, standard blowing in the wind and sword in hand, fighting the powerful Austrian army with his courageous troops and forging the victory. At the 1801 Salon, the painter Jean-Antoine Gros would exhibit his famous *Bonaparte au pont d'Arcole,* in which the general's pose is reminiscent of classical depictions of goddesses (body facing forward, torso and head turned to the left). The myth of Napoléon was truly "born on the plains of Italy." (Jean Tulard)

Bonaparte's triumphant entry into Milan

On Sunday, May 15, 1796, Bonaparte left his headquarters in Lodi for the Lombard capital, which had been occupied the previous day by French troops under General Masséna. At the Porta Romana Bonaparte mounted his white horse and entered the city. That evening he presided over a grand banquet, during which he confided to Marmont, his aide-de-camp, "Nowadays, no one conceives of anything great. It is for me to present an example."

"The Republic of France, which has pledged hatred toward tyrants, has also pledged fraternity with the people. This principle, which the republican Constitution has made hallow, is also that of the Army…. Respect for property, for individuals; respect for the religion of the people; these sentiments are those of the Government of the Republic of France and the victorious Army of Italy."

Proclamation of Bonaparte to the people of Lombardy, May 19, 1796

peninsula, he defined the politics of occupation without asking for advice from the Directory.

His independence reached its apogee when he alone negotiated the Treaty of Campoformio of October 18, 1797, by which Austria ceded to France control of Italy and the territory west of the Rhine. The Directory was forced to ratify the treaty to prove to the public its desire for peace; it also turned a blind eye to the "royal" practices of Mombello, as some of the spoils of war

Bonaparte took great riches from Italy for himself and his family. The confiscation of works of art was one of the most controversial aspects of the 1796–1797 campaign. (Right: the arrival of antiques into Paris, depicted on a Sèvres vase.) Above: During the same period the general, as if to atone, ordered the restoration of many masterpieces, one of which was Leonardo da Vinci's *The Last Supper*.

amassed by Bonaparte had made their way to France, alleviating its depleted finances.

In Paris the royalists swept the legislative elections, and the Directory's republican majority prepared a takeover by force to loosen the stranglehold. On July 14, 1797, Bonaparte chose his camp. He ordered General Augereau to "go to Paris and put himself in service to Barras." On September 4 (18 Fructidor) Bonaparte's envoy became the armed wing of the coup d'état.

Saved, the Directory faced another dilemma—what to do with Bonaparte, who did not want to continue his Italian sojourn? Barras convinced his colleagues to entrust him with an army to invade England.

"From the heights of these pyramids, forty centuries look down upon us!"

Bonaparte's return to France was triumphant. The people cheered; those who wanted to restore the directorial regime received him. Bonaparte was tempted to try a coup d'état, but judged the situation insufficiently ripe. He recognized quickly that the plans to "descend upon" England were destined to failure. With the support of Charles-Maurice de Talleyrand, the foreign minister, he suggested instead the conquest of

"The million for Toulon that I announced leaves tomorrow; another million, of which 500,000 francs is in gold, and as much in silver, leaves tomorrow for Paris. It will be used to revitalize our navy in Brest…, this with the addition of a million for the army at Sambre-et-Meuse, the same amount for that of the Rhine, 500,000 francs for that of the Alps, and the 500,000 francs that Corsica will cost us, will equal a sum of seven million that the Army of Italy will have furnished during this new campaign. The Pope has given us eight million diamonds that are worth at least 4,500,000 francs."

Bonaparte to
the Directory
May 14, 1797

Egypt, which would cut off England's route to India. He also understood that he had to distance himself from the plots fomenting in Paris and wait for his moment.

The Directory accepted the Egyptian plan—bidding Bonaparte "good riddance," one might add. In mid-May 1798, 54,000 men embarked on a dangerous Mediterranean crossing through waters dominated by English squadrons.

Bonaparte's army took Malta on June 10. On July 2 it occupied Alexandria after a battle that revealed the military incompetence of the Mamelukes (a military class descended from Caucasian slaves converted to Islam), who had gained political

"Pacification" also came to pass through example. Above: a plea for mercy from Sheik al-Fayoum, member of the Grand Divan, which Bonaparte denied (23 Frimaire Year VII, December 13, 1798).

control of Egypt, then nominally held by a weak Ottoman Empire.

Bonaparte's next destination was Cairo, and he chose the shortest route to reach it, which meant crossing the desert. Bonaparte led his men into hell. For twenty days, the young veterans of the revolutionary wars suffered from the heat of the day and the cold of the night. On July 21, they came upon the pyramids.

The Battle of the Pyramids was a disaster for the Mamelukes. Six thousand of them, astride magnificent horses adorned in gold but backed by only a few pieces of artillery, fell to Bonaparte's army. Lower Egypt was under Bonaparte's control. Victorious, his Army of Egypt entered Cairo, but there learned of a disaster at Aboukir: On August 1, in a bay near Alexandria, the British admiral Horatio Nelson had surprised a French fleet and trounced it. The Mediterranean was under English control, and the Army of Egypt was landlocked.

"All the Mamelukes, mounted upon splendid horses richly adorned in gold and silver, covered in draperies of all colors and flowing scarves, set off at full gallop, slashing the air with their cries, seeming as if, in the blink of an eye, they would annihilate us beneath their horses' hooves. Furthermore, no sooner than the order to fire was made was it executed, with a quickness and precision not possible during exercises or parades. Never had the battlefield produced a comparable spectacle. The order to fire had been made at such point-blank range that the tips of our rifles hooked onto the clothes of many Mamelukes and there fired, so that the perimeters of our square formation presented a spectacle of cadavers roasting in their clothes. The fat that ran over their limbs and on this fire fueled and spread a hideous odor."
The Battle of the Pyramids recounted by Colonel François Savary in his *Memoirs of the Duke of Rovigo.*

"I must be where my presence could be of the greatest use."

As he had done in Italy, Bonaparte organized the country and his administration, notably creating the Institute of Egypt, which he founded with numerous scholars whom he had brought with him from France. However, his efforts did not prevent the people of Cairo, who were spurred on by Turkish agents and adherents of the jihad, from rising up against the French occupation in October 1798. The insurrection was quelled in blood. Meanwhile, Upper Egypt was conquered by French troops under General Desaix.

The Army of Egypt was accompanied by a scientific expedition whose most prestigious scholars were inducted into the Institute of Egypt, where Bonaparte liked to spend time learning and debating. The scholars would bring back from their expedition valuable information about the ancient civilization, as well as many observations and concrete inventions. Left: Bonaparte depicted in the uniform of the members of the Institute.

The Ottoman Empire directed two armies against the French—one in Syria and the other in the outlying regions of Alexandria. Bonaparte first set out toward Syria, taking the cities of El-Alrich (February 20, 1799), Gaza (February 24), and Jaffa (March 7) in brutal battles. But the French could not seize Saint Jean d'Acre, the Syrian seaport. The troops were exhausted and disturbed—the plague had appeared among their ranks. Bonaparte had to evacuate the Holy Land.

With Syria lost, he still had to fight the second Ottoman army in Egypt. On July 25, 1799, his Army of Egypt crushed the Ottomans at the Battle of Aboukir.

But the news from France was bad. The demise of the Directory, both internally and on the foreign front, became manifest. Emmanuel-Joseph Sieyès, a member of the Directory, was preparing a coup. Bonaparte would have to return to France to take part. On August 23, with the utmost secrecy, he left Egypt, leaving his troops behind. Advantageous circumstances (and perhaps some complicity on the part of the English) enabled him to evade the enemy squadrons and to disembark near Fréjus on the Côte d'Azur on October 9, 1799.

Jean-Antoine Gros's painting *Bonaparte visitant les pestiférés de Jaffa* (*Bonaparte Visiting Plague Victims in Jaffa;* opposite) was presented at the 1804 Salon. The general-in-command is seen touching the sores of army plague victims. This painting, commissioned by Napoléon, served to erase the memory of the 3,500 prisoners his army massacred on the beaches of the city, as well as the abandonment of the plague victims (were they given opium?) when the army retreated.

J ust three weeks after his return from Egypt Bonaparte took part in the coup d'état that brought an end to the Directory. Two months later he was appointed first consul of the new regime. But he would still have to battle enemies from both without and within before gaining sole control of the management of affairs and climbing the steps to the imperial throne.

CHAPTER TWO
THE CONQUEST OF POWER
(1799–1804)

B y age twenty-six Napoléon Bonaparte wanted power. He neither hesitated nor applied scruples. By age thirty he had seized it, to the resounding applause of a bewildered populace. He then struggled to keep and expand his power. At age thirty-five he succeeded Charlemagne as emperor. Right: Returning from Egypt, he disembarked at Fréjus on October 9, 1799; left: in uniform as first consul.

"My entire part in the execution plot was limited to meeting, at the set hour, my throng of visitors and marching at their head in order to seize power."

According to Napoléon's recounting of the coup d'état of 18 Brumaire Year VIII (November 9, 1799), its execution was simple. Neither maneuvers nor negotiations had been needed. As if they had recognized him to be the most capable among them, those wishing to

Bonaparte at the Council of Five Hundred: a short spell of military fever in the middle of a parliamentary coup d'état. The writer Curzio Malaparte called it the "first modern coup d'état."

regenerate the Republic had rallied around him without encountering any opposition. But the matter was not that simple.

When he arrived in Paris on October 16, 1799, Bonaparte had the will to act, by force if necessary. But returning from Alexandria with several aides-de-camp, he was in charge of no command. To act he needed to control the Paris garrison, and such power could only be granted him by accomplices in the government. To gain some time he decided to ally himself with Sieyès and to appropriate the conspiracy he had set in motion a month earlier.

On 18 Brumaire Year VIII (November 9, 1799), on the pretext of countering a Jacobin plot, Sieyès succeeded in convincing the chambers of the Directory to name Bonaparte the head of the Paris garrison and to relocate their sessions to the Château de Saint-Cloud, far from the Parisian crowds and under the "protection" of the army. The following day the conspirators attempted to obtain from the two assemblies a change in the constitution, which they judged as the only way to save the Republic. With the debate going on endlessly, a haranguing Bonaparte tried to bring the lower house, the Council of Five Hundred, to a decision. The deputies rushed at him and he was removed from the meeting hall, protected by soldiers. Utterly unacquainted with the workings of political assemblies, he lost his sangfroid. It was his brother Lucien Bonaparte, president of the Five Hundred for merely a week, who handled the matter. Addressing the assemblage, he swore "to stab the breast of [his] own brother" if one day he attacked liberty. Regaining his composure, Napoléon ordered the forced evacuation of the meeting hall.

Following this bout of fever, the parliamentary coup d'état regained its momentum. With a handful of deputies united, the chambers suspended the constitution of the Directory and named three provisional consuls (Sieyès, Bonaparte, and Pierre-Roger Ducos), assigning them the task of drawing up a new constitution.

Sieyès planned the Brumaire coup but was not a man of action. He paid heavily in the months that followed and would brood over his regrets during a privileged retirement.

During a heated moment of the coup, Lucien Bonaparte provided his brother decisive assistance, but his ambition quickly became an encumbrance to Bonaparte.

"In a state like France, all harsh measures must come from the center."

On 20 Brumaire Year VIII (November 11, 1799) France, indifferent to the numerous coups d'état that had interrupted its political life during the past five years, was reawakened by the appearance of the Consulate in the place of the Directory. But its problems were not quickly resolved. France neither had a government nor any public finances. And Sieyès, Bonaparte, and Ducos had no clear political plans, having avoided addressing such questions during their preparatory meetings.

From their first sessions, the consuls were at odds. Ducos took Bonaparte's side. Patiently the general spun his web, backed by other accomplices of the coup d'état, such as Talleyrand, Joseph Fouché, and Jean-Jacques-Régis de Cambacérès. The professional classes stated their desire for a strong government. Instead of Sieyès, a theoretician, they preferred Bonaparte, who had supreme control over the army, the Republic's only organized military force, which he had already begun to purge.

Sieyès was eliminated gently and through his own instrument: the constitution. Bonaparte left him to define the broad outlines of the organization of power, intervening only on essential measures. When the constitution was proclaimed on December 13, he emerged as the great victor of the muted struggles begun the month before.

The new regime was republican. The executive office was awarded to three consuls, two appointed for ten years (Bonaparte and Cambacérès) and one for five years (Charles-François Lebrun). But at the last minute Bonaparte decided to take control as "First" Consul. The legislature was composed of two chambers—the Tribunate and the Legislative Body. A Senate, composed of appointed members, had only constitutional powers. Real power rested with the executive branch, supported by the Council of State (whose members were appointed

The new regime's Council of State, presided over by the first consul, was a brilliant assembly of specialists faithful to him. During his installation at the Petit Luxembourg Palace (right), Bonaparte, flanked by Cambacérès and Lebrun, receives the oath from the presidents of the sections—Boulay de La Meurthe (Legislation), Roederer (Interior), Defermon (Finances), Brune (War), and Ganteaume (Navy).

Bonaparte, Cambacérès, and Lebrun, the three consuls of the Republic. Bonaparte shared the executive office with a regicide and a moderate royalist. The two men were "wise, capable, but utterly opposite in politics," Napoléon would say.

by the executive office). A few weeks after the adoption of the constitution, a plebiscite was organized, and the approval was resounding. But the results were so greatly "rectified" by the minister of the interior, Lucien Bonaparte, that it is impossible to know the opinion of the French people.

The Consulate would remain the governing body of France until May 18, 1804, the date of the proclamation of the Empire. These four years were not to be a restful period for Bonaparte, who began solidifying his power by systematically eliminating his adversaries.

"We find ourselves in a position to conclude a solid peace, and if our enemies blindly oppose it, to embark upon a brilliant and decisive campaign to bring rest to Europe."

Soon after the Brumaire coup d'état, the situation on the foreign front improved. The French army had taken up

Charles-Maurice de Talleyrand-Périgord (1754–1838) was among those who brought Napoléon to power. He became minister of foreign affairs on November 22, 1799. He fell from grace in 1807, but continued to advise the emperor before betraying him in 1814.

the offensive again, winning some important victories, like the September 25–27, 1799, Battle of Zurich, at which General Masséna defeated the Russian forces. But while the Russians began to retreat from the western theaters, England and Austria remained steadfast in their decision to oppose the Revolution.

Even though he had not yet consolidated his power, Bonaparte had to lead an army in attack against the Austrians in Italy, while General Jean Moreau, commander-in-chief of the Army of the Rhine, conducted the offensive in Germany.

This second Italian offensive was shorter than that of 1796, but no less difficult. Using the element of surprise (no one expected that the Great Saint Bernard Pass through the Alps would be the chosen route, as it was still covered in snow), the advance guard of Marshal

Crossing the Alps by the Great Saint Bernard Pass (on donkeys rather than on temperamental horses) to surprise the Austrians, Napoléon wrote on May 18, 1800, to the consuls in Paris: "We are struggling with ice, snow, storms and avalanches. The [people] of Saint Bernard, astonished to see so many people cross so abruptly, presented a few obstacles. In three days, the whole army will have crossed."

Jean Lannes experienced some minor skirmishes before asserting its strength at the Battle of Montebello on June 9, 1800. Five days later, at Marengo, Bonaparte almost lost all, but was saved by the arrival on the battlefield of General Louis Desaix's division. (The general was killed during the battle.) The Austrian Army of Italy was no longer in any condition to cause trouble. On the German front, General Moreau's decisive victory at the Battle of Hohenlinden would not occur until December 3, 1800, but the primary external dangers had been contained, and peace was in the offing.

To the count of Lille: "You must not wish for your return to France; you will have to march over a hundred thousand corpses."

The problems from within were great. In the forefront of the opposition, the royalist "party"—in fact, a heterogeneous group favoring the return of the Bourbons—was reluctant to consider the first consul an enemy. Some hoped he would be the equivalent of the English general George Monck, who in 1660 had reestablished the monarchy following Cromwell's dictatorship.

However, the Brumaire coup's victors had republican natures. The regicides surrounding Bonaparte—represented by Cambacérès, his chief counselor, and Fouché, now the minister of police—did not have the slightest interest in the Bourbons' return.

The name Jacques-Louis David (1748–1825) is linked to Napoléon's. An arriviste, the painter supported this master as he had others, from the count d'Artois to Robespierre. He was responsible for many paintings that depicted, without concern for historical accuracy, the great moments of the era. If his *Bonaparte passant les Alpes au Grand Saint-Bernard* (*Bonaparte Crossing the Great Saint Bernard Pass*) is not his most famous work (see *La Sacre* / *The Coronation*), it was his "best seller." With his students, he painted five renditions, each with horses of a different color.

On his way to the Paris Opéra to attend a performance of Haydn's *Creation*, Bonaparte escaped an assassination attempt on Rue Saint-Nicaise in which two people were killed and six seriously injured (left and below). He accused the Jacobins. After an investigation using infiltrators and "scientific policing" to identify the owner of the mare harnessed to the carriage carrying the bomb, Minister of Police Fouché demonstrated that the royalists were responsible. Ultimately the two opposition parties in the Consulate were punished.

Two royalist temperaments were brewing: The politicians played the "Monck" card, and the men of action chose violence. The former, through their intermediary Talleyrand, tested Bonaparte. In response, the first consul asked if they would agree to join the "national" party he intended to lead. Numerous letters reached Paris from the count of Lille, the future Louis XVIII, pleading for the restoration of the throne, but none received a response. Finally, after the Battle of Marengo, Bonaparte took pen to hand, suggesting to the count of Lille that rather than having "to march over a hundred thousand corpses," he should instead "sacrifice his interests for the tranquility of France."

The "politicos" having failed, the men of action felt they had a free hand. The conspirators' primary objective was the physical elimination of Bonaparte. And they missed by only a hair. On December 24, 1800, the first consul escaped an assassination attempt when an "infernal machine" exploded as his carriage passed. For political reasons Bonaparte blamed the Jacobins, but Fouché convinced him that it was the royalists who sought his death.

Beyond such intrigues, problems were brewing throughout France. Armed gangs of bandits continually caused trouble in the west, and hired men launched a "small war" in the interior. General Jean-Baptiste-Jules Bernadotte received orders to cleanse the west of its *chouans* (counterrevolutionaries).

Only one implacable opposition remained.

"The art of being sometimes audacious and sometimes very prudent is the art of success."

There is a tendency to believe that following the Brumaire coup Napoléon's only enemies were foreign powers and royalists. The fractures of the Revolution were not, however, healed with a stroke of a magic wand. The Republican party comprised opposing sympathies, from the moderates to the Jacobins, from those partial to a concentration of power to those favoring a parliamentary democracy, from supporters of an appeasement regarding religious matters to adversaries

The pacification of the west of France, in a state of revolt since 1793, was one of the great, early successes of the Consulate. Alternating between carrot and stick, negotiations and a return to hostilities, a pardon for the repentant and severe sanctions against the implacable, Bonaparte managed to convince the majority of the populace—exhausted from eight years of civil war and repeated military losses—of his good will, notably through his policy of religious conciliation. In this engraving, part of the Histoire de France series the emperor commissioned in 1805, he is shown being warmly greeted by some defecting *chouans*.

of all religious sects. Bonaparte had to cross swords with the Republican oppositionists gathered around Fouché (a reputed Jacobin), Talleyrand (a moderate drawn to some kind of return of the ancien régime), Benjamin Constant (a supporter of liberalism), the ideologues of the Institut de France, the French academic society, members of the Tribunate (a chamber that did not

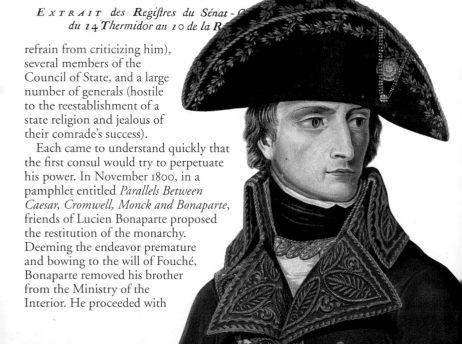

NAPOLEON
BONAPARTE
PREMIER CONSUL A VIE

SÉNATUS-CONSULTE

EXTRAIT des Registres du Sénat - C
du 24 Thermidor an 10 de la R

With religious peace, foreign peace, and a general amnesty for émigrés, 1802 was for Napoleonic France a "year without equal." Bonaparte was thirty-three years old (below) and all was well. The people had handed him a vote of confidence in a plebiscite. All political, economic, and social indicators pointed in the same direction: The French loved him and were happy. Left: text from the senatus consultum of 24 Thermidor Year X that made Bonaparte consul for life.

refrain from criticizing him), several members of the Council of State, and a large number of generals (hostile to the reestablishment of a state religion and jealous of their comrade's success).

Each came to understand quickly that the first consul would try to perpetuate his power. In November 1800, in a pamphlet entitled *Parallels Between Caesar, Cromwell, Monck and Bonaparte*, friends of Lucien Bonaparte proposed the restitution of the monarchy. Deeming the endeavor premature and bowing to the will of Fouché, Bonaparte removed his brother from the Ministry of the Interior. He proceeded with caution in matters requiring compromise and capitulation before the left, but also with fierce confrontation. He sent to the guillotine four Jacobin leaders implicated in the "conspiracy of the daggers" whose goal was to assassinate him.

Later he would not hesitate to confront the former revolutionaries who rebelled and spoke against the Concordat, the amnesty for émigrés, and the creation of the Legion of Honor. He would resist the urgings of the Council of State, the Legislative Body, and the Tribunate regarding the Civil Code, and he would rid himself of bothersome generals by offering them ambassadorships or secondary posts. He would go on the offensive against recalcitrant chambers, achieving a purge in March 1802, when a good portion of the Republican opposition was rooted out from official institutions.

"So as to insure the stability of our nascent institutions, to distance the citizen's gaze from the specter of discord, friends of the motherland have bestowed consulate for life upon the head of the supreme magistrate."

In the spring of 1802 Bonaparte held the various state entities in the palm of his hand. On May 6 of that year the post-purge Tribunate expressed its wishes to give him "a striking token of national recognition." The Senate approved a ten-year extension of his mandate, but he wanted more: perpetual power, a hereditary line. The Council of State gave its approval only for a plebiscite to ask the people if they wanted a consulate for life. The results of the plebiscite, announced on August 2, 1802, were outstanding. With a strong participation, there were 3,653,600 "yes" votes and 8,272 "no" votes. A month later Fouché, who had attempted to oppose the operation, was divested of his post at the Ministry of Police.

On June 19, 1802, while Joséphine was taking the waters at Plombières, Napoléon wrote, "I love you as the first day, because you are fine and, above all, lovable. A thousand lovable things and a kiss of love." Bonaparte was already upset about not having a child, but this man who did not like new ideas did not yet think of divorce. Below: the first consul and Joséphine strolling at the Château de Malmaison.

The Château de Malmaison, bought by Joséphine while Napoléon was in Egypt, was surrounded by a vast 640-acre (260-hectare) estate. The first consul liked to go there to relax or work, far from the Tuileries (his official residence since spring 1800). He installed a small office-library and a council room. When not dedicated to official duties, life there was typical of country sojourns. With a reduced staff, the mistress of the house, an expert at salons and entertainments (above), saw to events. After their divorce in 1809 Joséphine retreated to the château, where she died in 1814. Napoléon spent a few days there after Waterloo and prior to surrendering to the English. Today the grounds are smaller, but the château, transformed into a national museum in 1927, presents to the visitor an impressive collection.

The march toward an empire was on. It accelerated in August, when another change to the constitution authorized Bonaparte to name his successor. Gradually the idea of the monarchy was accepted among the populace and imposed upon the reticent faction of the consul for life's entourage. Several seemingly harmless measures alarmed Bonaparte's now powerless opponents,

including the creation of ladies-in-waiting around Joséphine, court mourning of the death of General Leclerc (Pauline Bonaparte's husband), the appearance of Bonaparte's profile on coins, the erection of a statue of Charlemagne at the Place Vendôme, and the reestablishment of the office of governor of Paris (to the benefit of Joachim Murat, Caroline Bonaparte's husband). And then the "great conspiracy" of 1804 allowed Bonaparte to take the last step between him and the throne.

Cadoudal and his accomplices were guillotined on June 28, 1804 (top). Three months before, the duke of Enghien was convicted and executed at the Château de Vincennes (above). In the same affair, Bonaparte exiled his rival General Moreau.

"I had the duke of Enghien arrested and judged because such was necessary for the security, interests and honor of the French people. In a similar circumstance, I would do the same."

The affair began early in 1804. The police unveiled an ambitious conspiracy led by the *chouan* leader Georges Cadoudal: Bonaparte was to be abducted along the route to his country house in Malmaison while a "prince" would enter the land and reestablish the monarchy.

Through a series of shaky deductions, it was concluded that the young duke of Enghien, a descendant of the Grand Condé (Prince Louis II de Bourbon), was the mysterious "prince." The duke was detained while, in Paris, Cadoudal and his accomplices were put behind bars. French soldiers arrested the duke; during the night of March 20–21, 1804, following a summary judgment, he was executed by firing squad at the Château de Vincennes.

The excuses of some historians notwithstanding, Bonaparte had wanted the duke of Enghien executed. The execution proved to be a founding act of the Empire—a definitive break with the Bourbons and an assurance to the revolutionaries. Climbing the scaffold, Cadoudal arrived at the same conclusion. "We had wanted to bestow upon France a king; we have given her an emperor."

"If our father had seen us!"

Satisfied with the twists taken by the affair and

Referring to the duke of Enghien, Talleyrand wrote, "[Napoléon] ascended a throne stained in the blood of the innocent." As did all the players in the affair, Talleyrand (whose own role was not slight) put the responsibility for it on others. Only Bonaparte accepted his. Below: the execution of the duke of Enghien at Vincennes.

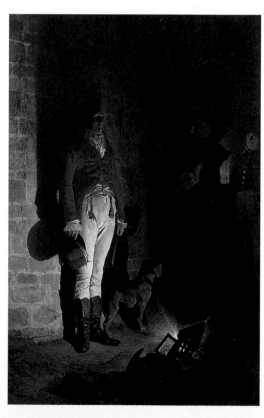

convinced that Bonaparte was unstoppable, the revolutionary left was behind the proclamation of the Empire from the outset. Senator Fouché, restored to grace, suggested to his assembly on March 27, 1804, that the first consul be invited "to finish his work by making it as immortal as his glory." A month later the Tribune Curée recommended that the Tribunate declare Napoléon Bonaparte emperor of France. After a three-day discussion, the motion was voted upon on May 3, 1804. Immediately the Council of State prepared a new constitution, which the Senate approved on May 18. In July the populace was finally consulted in a plebiscite; in a strong turnout, the people of France accepted the Empire, voting 3,572,329 in favor and 2,569 against.

The coronation of Napoléon I took place on December 2, 1804, in the Cathedral of Notre-Dame in Paris. Napoléon had wanted a lavish reception and succeeded in getting the pope to attend. However, the emperor crowned himself, with Pius VII merely reciting benedictions and an accolade to him. Napoléon then crowned Joséphine and took an oath, committing

The Senate vote (opposite, top: the results are presented to Napoléon) and the plebiscite (in which the people pronounced their opinion of heredity but not of the imperial principle) were capped by numerous symbolic ceremonies more than six months after the proclamation of the Empire (May 18, 1804). Two examples were the coronation on December 2 (opposite, below: a study for the famous painting by David) and the distribution of the Eagles statuettes to the army (above) at the Champs-de-Mars on December 5.

himself to the defense of France's borders, the equality of rights, civil and religious freedoms, the right of ownership, and the sale of national property. Thus, with the reiteration of the achievements of the Revolution, he concluded his coronation.

Two animals symbolized the Empire: the eagle (left, on the coronation sword) and the bee. Following lively debate and the advice of the Council of State (which had suggested the rooster), Napoléon's choice was made official by decree on July 10, 1804. The eagle (representing Antiquity) drew inspiration from Rome but also evoked Charlemagne, who used it in the ninth century. It appeared on seals, acts and official papers, buildings, dignitaries' attire, and regimental flagpoles. On the sword hilt here, the eagle clutches in its left claw the fasces of Jupiter (without the bolt of lightning). The bee was adopted upon after Cambacérès pointed out the communal insect's worker character and its prior use by the Merovingians. (In fact, the Merovingian dynasty, reigning from about 500 to 750, used cicadas, not bees, as a symbol.)

In less than fifteen years, Napoléon stabilized and reorganized a France bloodied by the Revolution. Not a single realm of the art of governance escaped his creative genius and his desire to control the synthesis of society's deep aspirations. Even if his empire did not survive military defeat, it built a durable work around a few basic principles—national reconciliation, order, and authority.

CHAPTER THREE
THE FOUNDER OF CONTEMPORARY FRANCE (1799–1810)

Even today, he is everywhere. This pragmatic one who said to himself, "submit to the dictatorship of circumstances," built an enduring work. He did not do it alone—his ministers, consuls of state, and dignitaries were the greatest practical thinkers of the day. He knew how to spur them on and give them the means to succeed. He was the first modern head of state. Left: Napoléon in his coronation attire, his hand above the Civil Code; right: the medal of the Legion of Honor.

"I am national."

In Brumaire Year VIII (November 1799) Bonaparte inherited a France that was politically disintegrated, economically depleted, socially divided, and spiritually destroyed. Everything had to be reconstructed. The task was enormous. Fifteen years later, this France had been changed and, despite Waterloo, appeared to be solid and organized, even if it had not entirely overcome its internal conflicts. A maniac for pragmatism, Napoléon did not have a true doctrine. He proceeded without preconceived ideas but with methodical coherence, leaning upon some lasting political ideals, rejecting—often scornfully—the theories of "ideologues" who had, nevertheless, been his allies during the Brumaire coup.

His internal works were as impressive as his military victories, and more durable. So many institutions and concepts of societal organization that continue to comprise French infrastructure date from Napoleonic France. In a very short period, during a time when communications were still rudimentary, Napoléon and the men around him changed the country to its core.

Following the four fiery years of the Consulate, Bonaparte would without difficulty become Napoléon and the people of the Revolution would applaud the creation of a "fourth dynasty." Since he climbed his way to the throne, France had regained order and civil peace. The economy of the most populous country in Europe had improved, the crisis abated by several good crops and the return of trade. On the international front, France was feared and respected, but not loved. As war returned—and the emperor was far from his capital with increasing frequency—his administration continued to reorganize and apply the "master's" directives regardless of where his bivouac happened to be. His orders, sent from great distances, took considerable time to arrive in Paris and be carried out. His accomplishments were thus all the more laudable.

After 1807 Napoléon's regime became even further entrenched, having silenced the opposition and strengthened his hold of the throne, and he adopted the demeanor of an absolute monarch.

With 40 million inhabitants, 85 percent of whom were rural, the France of 1800 offered a distinct advantage to Bonaparte's recovery efforts: the power of numbers. Even discounting the territories appropriated by the Revolution in Belgium, along the Rhine, and in Switzerland, France was the most populous state in Europe, ahead of Russia (30 million), Austria (24 million), England (16 million), and Prussia (9 million). Above: a country family.

Never in its history did France see such a production of legal texts, decisions, and negotiations (internal as well as foreign) as during the first years of the Consulate, a period when Napoléon's genius was at its most spectacular. "He wants to do everything, he knows how to do everything, and he can do everything," his contemporaries said in amazement.

"The government cannot ask of foreigners that which it must obtain from national industry," said Napoléon. But despite his personal efforts, his economic results were mixed. In 1809, however, French industry reached a new peak. The value of its production rose 50 percent compared to 1789. Below: Napoléon visits a factory in Rouen.

"As Consul, my first thought had been to begin peace negotiations."

France had been at war with her neighbors since April 20, 1792. The Legislative Assembly, which governed the country in 1791–92 and had "declared world peace," led Europe into an interminable war with an uninterrupted chain of human and material sacrifice. To stabilize the Revolution, Bonaparte sought peace from the very start. His early overtures were rejected, but following the campaigns of 1800 an end to war became possible, without France having to concede its revolutionary-era conquests—the left bank of the Rhine and northern Italy.

Peace treaties appeared in succession: first with Austria (Peace of Lunéville, February 9, 1801), then with Naples (Peace of Florence, March 28, 1801), Russia (Peace of Paris, October 8, 1801), and, most important, with England (Peace of Amiens, March 25, 1802). These were complemented by accords with Spain (October 1, 1800, and March 21, 1801) and the United States (October 3, 1800). On June 25, 1802, when it signed a treaty with Turkey, France was at peace for the first time in ten years.

The impact of total peace was profound throughout the population. It was celebrated by both official festivities and by families who had endured the absence of their husbands and sons for many long years. Peace was a defining internal event of the beginning of the Napoleonic period; another was the 1801 signing of the religious Concordat.

The Treaty of Lunéville, signed with Austria, was greeted by widespread displays of joy supported by official celebrations (above). But the true success would be the end of the Franco-English war, a prerequisite for any hope for peace on the European continent. As a popular engraving (left) illustrates, the Peace of Amiens (signed with England) allowed Bonaparte to resheath his sword. It would remain sheathed for only fourteen months. The "Second One Hundred Years War" (Pierre Gaxotte, contemporary French historian), started by Louis XIV with the War of the League of Augsburg in 1688, would not come to an end until the Battle of Waterloo in 1815.

"If I were governing a Jewish nation, I would reestablish the Temple of Solomon."

Reconciling the French people without abandoning the principles of the Revolution (version 1789) was the challenge facing the men of the Brumaire coup. They would have to take repressive action against the obdurate and also make measures of appeasement—such as granting amnesty for émigrés (most of the "returnees" would rally around the regime) and reconstructing devastated regions (Lyon, the Vendée, Brittany, etc.).

In this allegorical painting celebrating the Peace of Amiens, Bonaparte is being bestowed with a laurel wreath while awaiting the imperial crown.

But at the most profound level it was society's gaping wound of religious discord that needed healing. The government had been at odds with the Catholic Church since its revolutionary confiscation of church property and rejection of the pope's authority. After ten years the French, more than 90 percent of whom practiced Catholicism before 1789, were tired of revolutionary sects persecuting priests and occupying churches.

Loi du

Article C

Napoléon viewed religions in the context of public order. They had to be organized and controlled by the state. For Protestants (above: the law organizing Protestantism) and, above all, for Jews (left), the provision of a legal status, however severe, was viewed as an acknowledgment by the state and a great moment in their history.

The Concordat was negotiated between Rome and Paris without delay. Signed on July 15, 1801, it was ratified in August by the pope and in September by Bonaparte, who had to fight opposition in the chambers, purge the Tribunate, and force the Legislative Body to vote for the text on April 8, 1802. The accord was solemnly proclaimed at Notre Dame on Easter Sunday, April 18.

The Concordat restored a position to Catholicism ("the religion of the great majority of the French people") but did not grant it the status of

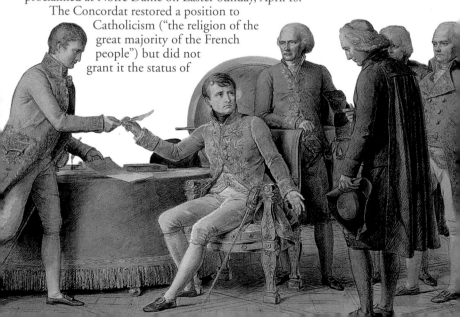

18 Germinal an 10.

ganiques des Cultes Protestans.

a state religion, as it had been under the ancien régime. Places of worship were returned to the church, and the state agreed to pay clerics' salaries. In exchange, the nomination of archbishops, bishops, and parish priests was to be made by the government; those the pope then chose were obliged to take an oath of loyalty to the Republic.

It was of little importance to the people that this Concordat was imperfect, or that the two parties' disagreements would eventually rise to such a pitch that Pope Pius VII would excommunicate Napoléon, who in turn would have him arrested in 1809. What did matter was the return to freedom of religion and religious peace.

In restoring some rights to Roman Catholicism, Napoléon was not committing an act of piety, merely political necessity. As he would explain in his last years, "Religious ideas still have greater hold than some short-sighted philosophers believe; they can render a great service to humanity. Being in good [standing] with the pope, one rules even today over the consciences of a hundred million men." In the same vein and upon founding the laic state, he would grant a status to the Protestant religion (1802) and adopt legislation favorable to Jews (1808).

"I have wanted to realize in a state of forty million individuals that which was done in Sparta and Athens."

Organizing the nation was Napoléon's primary ambition. As Pierre Louis Roederer, the politician who was one of his Brumaire accomplices, wrote, "Order! There is the

On this engraving announcing an Easter Mass to be attended by the three consuls on April 18, 1802, the artist, evoking Bonaparte, included a phrase from the Canticle of the Blessed Virgin: "He hath showed might with His arm; He hath scattered the proud in the conceit of their heart."

Imposed upon ideologues and republicans, the Concordat, along with the amnesty for émigrés, was the cornerstone of national reconciliation. Opposite: Bonaparte signing the text of the Concordat.

true object of the Constitution, the task of every government, the essence of all public prosperity." To attain such an ideal, Bonaparte undertook first to concentrate authority, then to organize the administration and the political and social institutions. Throughout, he opted for a pyramid structure, of which he was the pinnacle.

"The principle was rigor; the goal, order; and the methods, authoritarian," wrote author Frédéric Bluche. The law of Pluviôse Year VIII (February 1800) was the nucleus of the plan and the most outstanding illustration of the concern for rationalization. The law simplified and made uniform the administration, transforming the election of local representatives into a mere souvenir of the Revolution. Local jurisdiction was

An annual exhibition of industrial products, founded in 1798, took place in 1801 (above). That year, in the courtyard of the Louvre, numerous inventions of lasting value debuted:

Conté presented his crayon, Bauwens his spun cottons, Deharme and Dubaux their varnished canvas, Jacquemart and Benard their painted papers, and Sèvres his porcelains.

placed in the hands of the prefect who, under the authority of the minister of the interior, exercised the activities of the state for his department. He represented the state, directed the department's administration, and supervised the district's lower divisions—the *arrondissement* and the *commune*. (The *commune* appointed mayors.) He also informed Paris of small and large events within his jurisdiction, oversaw public opinion, and was responsible for the public order.

This concern for reorganization was noticeable in all domains of the state: financial and economic institutions (creation of the Banque de France, stock market, revenue courts, and chambers of commerce; the introduction in 1803 of a new currency, the franc germinal; promotion of industrial products in official exhibitions; imposition of a state-fixed interest rate); fiscal policy (with a preference for indirect taxes collected by the formidable department of Droits Réunis); cultural institutions (expansion of the Louvre, reorganization of the Institut de France); central and decentralized administrations; the justice system (reorganization at all levels, from justices of the peace to the Supreme Court of Appeals; creation of notaries and labor conciliation boards); public instruction (creation of secondary schools in 1802 and the Imperial University in 1808); public works; and so forth.

"I want to lay upon the ground of France masses of granite."

Napoléon thought that the Revolution, by encouraging egotism and fratricidal fights

Every function in Napoleonic society had its own outfit or uniform, from the high judge, the minister of justice (opposite), to prefects (below), to schoolboys (left). While the uniforms could be seen as a desire for regimentation, Napoléon was in fact merely observing a tradition that persists today: Having a regulation outfit meant having a recognized status in society. Those who did not have one, such as the members of the Institut de France, felt denigrated. They readopted theirs and continue to wear it to this day.

The emperor promised the Legislative Body that Paris would be "the greatest capital in the universe." By the end of his reign the city had been modernized, with a new odd-even numbering system for addresses; the installation of fountains; and the development of cemeteries, squares, markets, wharfs and piers, and official palaces. Monuments such as the Louvre (which housed the Napoléon Museum; opposite) were enlarged. The Arc de Triomphe du Carrousel (above) was finished long before the one planned for the Champs-Elysées. Also erected were the Châtelet column (below), less well known than its counterpart at the Place Vendôme; statues of dignitaries and great men; the Passerelle des Arts (a walkway across the Seine); the Ile de la Cité bridge (since destroyed); and the Austerlitz and Iéna bridges. On the other hand, most of the projects begun were never completed, nor was the renovation of several neighborhoods.

among Frenchmen, furthered the dissolution of the society. To stabilize those who would become his co-citizens, he had to create institutions that would build the body social.

Bonaparte entrusted his top jurists (including Cambacérès, Jean-Etienne-Marie Portalis, and Félix Bigot de Préameneu) with the preparation and the implementation of an essential task—the codification of laws, beginning with civil laws. He personally participated in the discussions held before the Council of State and presided over 57 of the 102 sessions dedicated to the Civil Code. On March 21, 1804, after four years of work—and despite opposition by a sector of the chambers that deplored the abandonment of some revolutionary reforms—the government promulgated the Civil Code, comprising 36 laws and 2,281 articles. (In 1807 it would become the Napoleonic Code.) At the

The Legion of Honor was created in 1802. Depicted here is the bestowing two years later of the first "crosses," medals that were actually in the shape of stars. The organization of this structured institution constituted an important stage in the creation of a new elite class, which owed its status and recognition to the Napoleonic regime.

heart of this monument were ownership and family rights that, in many respects, have stood the test of time. Other codes would come into being throughout the duration of the Empire: Code of Civil Procedure (1806), Commercial Code (1807), Code of Criminal Procedure (1808), Penal Code (1810), and the Rural Code (1814).

To help govern the regional departments of France, the Napoleonic regime relied upon prominent people identified by the prefects on their "lists of notabilities." Seats were reserved for them on the district, national, and general councils (all advisory in nature). In return they were to federate the body social and assist the government. The notability took the place of elections as, thanks to earlier plebiscites and before soaking his legitimacy in a monarchical bath, the emperor considered himself the sole representative of the nation.

Whereas the Revolution had eliminated distinctions among classes, Napoléon decided to institute a national order that would acknowledge civil merit and military courage, as well as create a sort of chivalry that would regroup the elite of the country. And thus, by a decree of May 19, 1802, the Legion of Honor came into being.

The legion's first "crosses" (star-shaped medals affixed with a red ribbon) were presented two years later. The Empire would decorate some 35,000 people. Napoléon then created the imperial nobility on March 1, 1808. The honor was bestowed upon the emperor's closest associates and also tied privileged families, including those of the ancien régime, to his regime. In six years Napoléon would create

Through the efforts of Jean-Jacques-Régis de Cambacérès (1753–1824), one of the great jurists of his time and Napoléon's veritable "right hand" during the Consulate and the Empire (left), French laws were codified within ten years. Of course Napoléon was simply pursuing a goal of the Revolution. But successfully concluding the theoretical debates, proceeding to practical applications, and then creating a new legal order that synthesized traditional and revolutionary ideals was no mean accomplishment. The crown jewel of this effort was undoubtedly the Civil Code. Below: Napoléon's personal copy.

42 princes and dukes, some 500 counts, 1,550 barons, and 1,500 knights.

This new nobility would not unconditionally support the Empire. It would, however, come to constitute the base of a new noble and bourgeois elite in the 19th century.

"It is not by cajoling the people that one wins them over."

Confronted by the need to reestablish order and to impose national reconciliation, Napoléon concentrated all state authority in his own hands. Imperceptibly, the opposition abdicated, the collaborators yielded, and the inevitable flatterers cheered him. A few purges of the chambers, the administrations, and even of the army resolved the most extreme crises. The imperial Constitution of 1804 confirmed a truth perceived since the Consulate—Napoléon alone was the "Government."

The product of a coup d'état backed by the bourgeoisie, the Napoleonic regime— whose popular attributes disappeared after 1804— paid back the bourgeois class for its support. Society was sculpted around the idea of "notability"—from the lists of eligibility, trust, and taxation used to choose servants of the state to the imperial nobility granted by the sovereign. After 1807–8, the Revolution was over. Above: the outer ornaments and distinctive shield of the French grand dukes following the March 1, 1808, imperial decree.

While his power became more consolidated, the master became "prickly" (Fouché) and strengthened the apparatus of societal controls. Napoléon would always be convinced that the French were more concerned with equality than with liberty, and in this he was not wrong. But contrary to long-standing opinion, his regime was not a "military" dictatorship. Certainly the organization was based upon military models (a hierarchical pyramid that relied on obedience), and the army was an absolute pillar of the Empire. But the principles were set in motion by a civil administration to which the military was subordinate.

According to those around him, the emperor was "the most civil of military men."

Napoléon did not, however, practice the political liberalism that myth claims. The press was regulated, rationed, and censured. Literary and theatrical pieces, including classic works, were censored and cleansed. The police, first under Fouché and then under Savary, were omnipresent, and justice was harsh. In 1810 state prisons, where the opposition could be incarcerated without trial, were created. Their

Antiquity was a point of reference for the regime, in its terminology (consul, prefect), symbols (the eagle), and discourse. Below: dignitaries in a "Roman setting."

impact might best be understood by statistics: 1,500 people would be imprisoned there. Finally, the prohibition of associations and the creation of the workers' passbook in 1804 restricted and kept a watch over the working class.

This permanent supervision over the citizenry was indispensable to many imperial demands, especially as discontentment among the population grew. Among the regime's unpopular moves was a return to war soon after the declaration of peace. War would take the emperor far from a capital he could entrust (and only somewhat) to just one person, and it instigated a conscription that progressively ate up France's young men. ("I have one hundred thousand men in stock," Napoléon said on one of his bad days.) To address the needs of a war economy, public finances relied on a system of heavy taxation and an administration that mercilessly collected it. The government's watchful eye meant to suppress dissent over such moves and ensure that old rivalries born of the Revolution did not reemerge from its ashes.

Despite the occasional riot and popular outcry (mainly directed against the military conscription), the policy of order and authority was well accepted. Carefully coordinated propaganda and constant supervision alone do not explain the French people's attachment to the monarch and his regime (at least until the Russian campaign of

s'adresser, pour les abonnemen
Chef du Bureau de la *Gazette*, r

GAZ

A contemporary of Savary, the minister of police (1810–14), stated, "If the emperor told him to kill you, he would have taken you by the hand and said, 'I despair to send you off to the other world; the emperor wishes it so.'" Below: Savary.

. STÉVENIN ;
istine, n° 5.

Prix, 14 l. pour trois mois ; 27 l. pour six mois ; 54 l.
pour l'année. (Les lettres doivent être affranchies.)

(N° 3014)

TTE DE FRANCE

MERCREDI, 23 AVRIL 1806.

Approuvé   Projet de Décret.

Napoléon, Empereur des Français,

Roi d'Italie, Protecteur de la Confédération
du Rhin, Médiateur de la Confédération
Suisse, &c. &c. &c. :

De la Direction et Surveillance du Théâtre Français.

Art. 1er

Le Théâtre français continuera d'être placé sous
la Surveillance et la Direction du Surintendant de nos
Spectacles.

1812). The population, which was predominantly rural, appreciated the restoration of prosperity and was grateful to Napoléon for having solidified the right of ownership, guaranteed that profits gained from national goods (the fruit of revolutionary confiscations from the clergy and the nobility) would revert to the public domain, reestablished religion,
won the war against banditry, and created an educational system that was significantly more accessible than before.

Joseph Fouché (1759–1820), regicide, Jacobin, and minister of police (1799–1802, 1804–10, and during the Hundred Days of 1815), was the founder of modern police methods. Fouché (above) exercised power over workers (opposite: the workers' passbook), the press (top), and the Théâtre Français (left). He betrayed the emperor in 1815. Though Fouché favored the return of Louis XVIII, the king would not acknowledge him and sent him into exile.

The success of his "Grande Armée" made Napoléon a conqueror without equal, without precedent—a "God of War," according to Carl von Clausewitz, a Prussian army officer. Austerlitz, Jena, Friedland, Wagram—Napoléon's victories are famous throughout the world. The Napoleonic Wars were both a continuation of France's revolutionary wars and the climax of the Franco-English rivalry for domination of the continent.

CHAPTER FOUR
THE GOD OF WAR
(1800–1810)

Napoléon understood the changes in the art of war and put them to action. With soldiers of the Revolution, he conquered Europe before sacrificing his achievements to his ambition. Left: Napoléon at the height of his glory; right: his military kit.

"I never made war with a mind to conquer; I accepted the wars that the English minister waged against the French Revolution."

Until the Peninsular War in Spain (1808) this justification, as Napoléon expressed it, was indisputable. France's enemies viewed the Consulate as no more than a new phase of revolutionary movement. The proclamation of Empire did little to change their positions. Instead of a government of "terrorists," Europe's monarchies faced an "upstart" regime, which, after the death of the duke of Enghien, was no better than its regicidal predecessor. From his point of view, Napoléon had vowed to hold on to the Republic's previous conquests—the left bank of the Rhine and northern Italy.

To the rest of Europe, Napoléon continued to be the beneficiary of the great upheaval of 1789, but the Napoleonic Wars must also be viewed from the perspective of a Franco-English rivalry. Crucial economic and diplomatic interests were at stake. A powerful France would eliminate any possibility of England ever playing a political or commercial role on the continent. For its part France had many scores to settle—including the loss to England of India and Canada (1763) and, after 1792, numerous other colonies.

"War with England would be eternal if it opened a single opportunity for its commerce."

The two key players in the European conflict had few means to strike each other directly. England dominated the seas. It could impose what its prime minister, William Pitt, called "an English war," which entailed economic measures and sudden strikes in the colonies and against enemy and neutral ships. On land, however, British forces were no match for the larger and more war-hardened Napoleonic army. Not until 1808, during the Peninsular War in Spain, would England partake in a land operation. Prior to that England was the foundation of the anti-French coalition, waging war by proxy, fueling the slightest conflict between France and the other continental powers, and financing the war effort.

To combat England, Napoléon sought to divide the coalitions. He first envisioned sharing Europe with Russia, then attempted a dynastic alliance with Vienna. He would try to ally with the United States, but the Anglo-American War of 1812 came too late to help France. His only weapon against London was economic warfare. French caricatures (above) show the potential progressive effects of a commercial blockade. But his political alliances, invasions, and insufficient naval power prevented him from ever enforcing a complete blockade.

France and England engaged in a merciless war of caricatures, from which England emerged the victor. Bonaparte's impetuousness and small size were ridiculed on the other side of the Channel. The famous cartoonist James Gillray depicted him (below) as Gulliver standing on the palm of King George III, who pronounces him "one of the most pernicious, little odious reptiles."

England's economic health and its diplomatic ability, which would unite all of Europe against France, would also save the throne of George III, despite his loss of the American colonies and opposition to his reign.

Under Napoléon France would again prosecute the economic war against England that first had been decreed during the Directory. Ten years had passed since either nation had used such a weapon when, in 1806, he instituted the "Continental System," a blockade meant to exclude British goods from Europe. This time the economic war would be total. England would just barely manage to retain its power.

It is difficult to say who broke the 1802 Treaty of Amiens after little more than a year

My little friend Grildrig you have made a most admirable panegyric upon Yourself and Country. but from what I can gather from your own relation & the answers I have with much pains wringed & extorted from you, I cannot but conclude you to be, one of the most pernicious, little odious reptiles that nature ever suffer'd to crawl upon the surface of the Earth —

of peace. England, by refusing to return Malta to France in September 1800, had given Napoléon a good pretext to take up the fight. On May 20, 1803, the two sides returned to a war that would last another eleven years.

Deciding that it was necessary to "seek peace in London," Napoléon undertook preparations for a landing on the British Isles. The Grande Armée—as the French army was still called—made camp in Boulogne. Crossing the Channel would take several days. The English navy was powerful, but the first consul had swept Spain into his wake, and the Franco-Spanish flotilla aspired to rival the enemy fleet. The timing was set: The descent upon England would take place between August 8 and 18, 1805.

But resentment was growing in the heart of Europe. Austria did not appreciate the transformation of a part of northern Italy into a kingdom with Napoléon as monarch. Russia, always quick to follow the policies of the English cabinet—which, with the complicity of locals, fomented the assassination of the Francophile Czar Paul I, who was replaced in 1801 by his son Alexander—joined this third coalition. The Kingdom of Naples soon followed. With this menace at his back, Napoléon abandoned his English plan. Austria soon invaded Bavaria, an ally of France, while a Russian army advanced westward.

"It will suffice you to say, 'I was at the Battle of Austerlitz,' for one to respond, 'There is a brave man!'"

On August 25, 1805, the emperor gave the order for the Grande Armée to leave its encampments in northwestern France and march toward the center of Europe. Within a few weeks the French had turned the tide. "Seven torrents" (columns of the French army) descended upon the Austrian troops of General Mack, which were vanquished in an attack led by Marshal Ney at Elchingen on October 14 and forced to surrender at Ulm on October 19 by Napoléon himself.

On November 14, 1805, Napoléon occupied Vienna, then pushed on to Moravia to finish off the Austro-Russian forces. By that point he no longer regretted having post-

In an "about-face," Napoléon transported his army from the camp at Boulogne (left) to the south of Germany (below: crossing the bridge over the Lech River at Augsburg on October 12, 1805) almost without being noticed. The Grande Armée encountered the Austrian army before the arrival of Russian reinforcements. The 1805 campaign demonstrated France's overwhelming superiority on land, compared to the coalition forces.

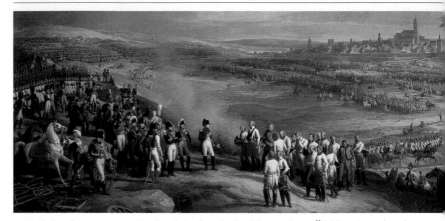

poned the descent upon England. In fact, he had learned that on October 21, 1805, the Franco-Spanish fleet, under the command of Admiral Villeneuve, had been destroyed off Cape Trafalgar by the English, under Admiral Nelson, who was killed in the battle. England was, and would remain for long thereafter, the master of the seas.

Napoléon did, however, remain indomitable on land. On the anniversary

of his coronation, December 2, 1805, in a now famous maneuver at Austerlitz, he crushed the Austro-Russian army commanded by General Kutusov, in the presence of the emperors of Austria and Russia. A triumph of Napoleonic tactics and a model taught in French military academies until the eve of World War I, this "battle of three emperors" established the moral and material annihilation of the conquered. Austria called for an armistice and signed the Treaty of Pressburg on December 26, 1805. A few months later France occupied the Kingdom of Naples and installed Joseph Bonaparte on its throne.

"Soldiers, I am pleased with you. Today, at Austerlitz, you have borne out all that I have heard of your fearlessness. You have decorated your eagles with immortal glory. My nation will look upon you with joy and it will suffice you to say, 'I was at the Battle of Austerlitz,' for one to respond, 'There is a brave man!'"
Proclamation at Austerlitz

"Monsieur the Minister of Police, you shall see to it that no more foolish remarks are said about Russia. Everything indicates that our system will join with this power in a stable manner."

The English and the Russians pursued the war, hoping to ally with Prussia, the last European power to offer its forces.

Napoléon presented the pretext for Prussia's entry into the coalition against France. In July 1806 he created the Confederation of the Rhine, proclaiming himself the protector of the minor German states. War fever seized the entourage of Prussia's King Frederick William III. On October 7, 1806, Napoléon received an ultimatum

At the Battle of Ulm 25,000 Austrians fell into French hands. This success (opposite) was overshadowed by the naval disaster at Trafalgar, where the outnumbered British fleet, under Admiral Nelson, won a resounding victory. Thirteen French and nine Spanish vessels were sunk.

This map of the campaigns of 1805, 1806–7, and 1809 retraces the offensives of the Grande Armée against the third, fourth, and fifth coalitions.

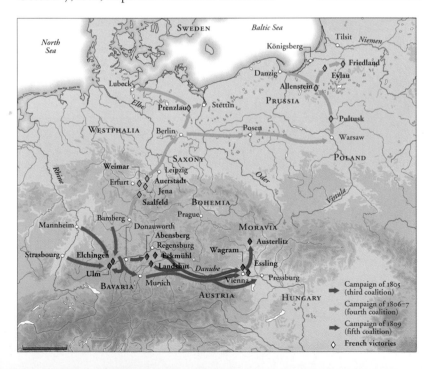

The victory at the Battle of Austerlitz ended the 1805 campaign "with a crash of thunder" (Edmond Rostand). Napoléon had chosen the Moravian battlefield to the southeast of Brno. In the days preceding the confrontation, he convinced the Austro-Russian forces (commanded by Kutusov, with the Austrian and Russian emperors at his side) that he was afraid of them, abandoning the best positions. He wanted to be attacked from his unprotected right, so as to envelop the enemy with his left flank. On December 2, 1805, while the "sun of Austerlitz" rose, the plan—continuously readapted—worked. The Austro-Russian forces did attack the French right front, but it was at the center that Bonaparte clinched his victory, driving the best enemy regiments onto the Pratzen Heights. By evening, General Rapp presented the captured flags to his commander (left). December 2 became a symbolic date for the Bonapartes: Napoléon's coronation, Austerlitz, the 1851 coup d'état, the proclamation of the Second Empire.

demanding his withdrawal from Germany. Saxony and Sweden joined the coalition.

The day after this demand expired Napoléon unleashed his most extraordinary campaign. The Grande Armée thrashed the Prussian troops in a number of battles—Saalfeld, Weimar, Jena, and Auerstadt. After the French occupation of Berlin on October 27, 1806, the pursuit of the remnants of the Prussian army took the form of a military procession punctuated by mass surrenders, with fortified towns and cities falling one after another. Marshal Joachim Murat wrote to the emperor, "The combat is over for want of combatants." But this was not completely true. The Russian army had arrived, and Poland would become the next theater of conflict.

Come December they would kill each other in Soldau, Pultusk, and Golymin. On February 8, 1807, Napoléon emerged the victor of an appalling butchery during a

Napoleonic propaganda demanded that the emperor's victory at Jena (below) eclipse the French army's victory at Auerstadt the same day.

In Friedland (left), the Russian army was defeated by Napoléon's tactical perseverance: Taking into account the enemy's imprudent crossing of the Alle River, the French doggedly cut off all exits. Once the three bridges crossing the river were destroyed, the Russians were trapped.

fierce snowstorm in Eylau, although a definitive resolution could not be reached. Fighting was suspended to regroup ranks bled dry by the winter campaign; then, with the first days of nice weather, the war resumed. On May 24, 1807, Danzig (modern-day Gdansk) fell to the French. On June 14 the Russian army, drawn into a trap by Napoléon, was trounced at the Battle of Friedland.

On June 25, 1807, Napoléon and Czar Alexander I made peace in Tilsit, leaving the king of Prussia on the sidelines. On July 7 the two emperors—who seemed to agree on the partitioning of the continent—signed the Treaty of Tilsit. Once again England stood alone against Napoléon.

"The art of war is a simple art; everything is in the performance. All is common sense, nothing is ideology."

The "God of War" did not invent a new strategy. Through study, reflection, and synthesis Napoléon became one of the great captains of the world. He had discovered his

Following the Treaty of Tilsit, the friendship between Napoléon and Czar Alexander was celebrated as a guarantee of peace. But the alliance was delicate and, with the pressure of events, would explode five years later. Above: the two sovereigns depicted on a watch.

Napoléon's Advance into Berlin

"We made our entry [into Berlin] by the Brandenburg Gate and the magnificent Unter den Linden Street. The emperor appeared there at the head of twenty thousand troops. The army was in full regalia, as radiant as at the Tuileries, and he, in his modest outfit, with a small hat bearing the national cocarde! Such a spectacle for those who could be with him! The inhabitants of Berlin were everywhere, and their admiration did not even compare to that of the Parisians upon our return from Austerlitz."

Captain Jean-Roch Coignet

"Our brigade entered Berlin at two o'clock in the afternoon. The city was beautiful, but sad. All the shops were closed. No one was at the windows, and few people were in the streets. There were no carriages. The only noise to be heard in the streets was from the artillery and the caissons of our army."

Commander Charles Parquin

Human statistics of the Napoleonic Wars

Between 600,000 and 1 million Frenchmen perished in the wars that raged between 1792 and 1815, about 75 percent of those deaths dating after 1805. Even those who did not die during the battles would continue to be haunted by their deadliness. The counts of French deaths illustrate the brutality of the battles, each of which lasted a single day: Austerlitz (1,200), Jena (5,000), Eylau (15,000), Friedland (7,000), Wagram (17,000), Moskowa (10,000), Leipzig (20,000), Ligny and Waterloo (20,000 to 25,000). France's enemies suffered even greater losses in most of these battles: Jena (12,000), Friedland (25,000), Wagram (20,000), Moskowa (20,000), Leipzig (35,000), Ligny and Waterloo (15,000). Contrary to wide belief, the revolutionary and imperial wars had little impact on French demography; the natural growth of the population was stronger between 1790 and 1816 than between 1740 and 1790. Left: Napoléon visiting the battlefield at Eylau.

strategy in the count de Guibert's writings on the campaigns of Frederick the Great, the king of Prussia (1740–86): War is movement; it is won on the legs of soldiers; to surprise the enemy, pursue him when he is beaten; position yourself safely in case of need.

Interminable forced marches, uncomfortable tents, overburdened health services, unreliable provisions—Napoléon did not concern himself with satisfying the basic needs of his troops. However, the "little corporal" was a born leader without equal. He knew how to play upon the emotions of the soldiers he called his own. Further, Napoléon had a generation of warriors at his disposal. France had been fighting since 1792. There was not an army in the world that had its soldiers' experience, nor one with so many superior officers. The military machine available to the emperor, in particular General Gribeauval's artillery system, was the best of its day.

Complementing his strategy of movement, Napoléon believed in seeking the quickest, most decisive battle possible. This was a departure from the 18th-century practice of siege as the principal method and battle as a final resort. Napoléon instead quickly engaged the enemy. Tactics varied according to the situation but were always in keeping with a rule he established in 1797: "The art of war consists, with an inferior army, of always having more strength than your enemy at the point of attack or the point of being attacked." The rest was a function of terrain, the opposing troops, and the campaign's objective. The emperor often decided the day's tactic in a sudden inspiration following a long meditation.

To command his army corps, Napoléon appointed twenty-six marshals of the Empire between 1804 and 1815, reestablishing a rank abolished in 1793. They had been chosen from "among the most distinguished generals," but some promotions were also designed to win over the regime's top guns (Bernadotte, Ney, Jourdan, Masséna, Augereau, Brune, et al.). Left, top to bottom: three marshals with different skills—Alexandre Berthier, organizer; Louis Nicolas Davout, tactician; and Jean Lannes, a brave friend, killed during the Battle of Essling.

In contrast to the usual Napoleonic field strategy, the Battle of Eylau (left) was a poorly prepared frontal attack. The French were outnumbered on all battlefields where maneuvers had ended. Noting this vulnerability, Napoléon ordered a pause in the campaign. Below: The emperor observes his enemy. At his side is Marshal Joachim Murat, grand duke of Berg, later king of Naples.

From 1805 to 1809 no general dared counter Napoléon's methods. It was simple guerrilla fighters who put his reputation on the line and, more important, began to dismantle the imperial edifice.

"Spain has long been the object of my thoughts."

All Napoléon's troubles would begin with his adventure in Spain, which arose from villainy and ended in disaster. Why did Napoléon ever get involved in his Spanish operation? He too would ponder that question toward the end of his life, from his home in exile on the island of Saint Helena.

King Carlos IV governed from Madrid with the aid of his favorite minister, Manuel

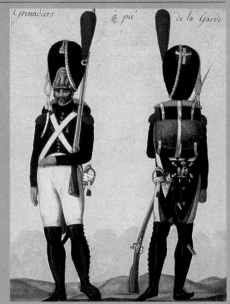

Artillerie à cheval

These watercolors, painted from life, accurately reproduce the appearance of soldiers of the Grande Armée in 1807. Top left: an officer of the Eighth Infantry Regiment wearing the shako and the yellow chamois collar, the color assigned to the infantry (an elite company of small, agile men capable of quick action). Top right: foot grenadiers of the Imperial Guard wearing their buttoned outfit (or *surtout,* a greatcoat for road and country). The plume was usually part of the dress uniform reserved for pageants, entry into enemy capitals, and important battles. The elite of the elite, the grenadier alone symbolized the Imperial Guard. Below left: a sapper of the Third Infantry Regiment. Products of the Royal Army, the sappers carried an axe, a musket, and a short sword. Their primary purpose was to destroy obstacles. Bottom right: an officer of the 24th Regiment of Chasseurs wearing a busby hat. Along with the hussars, the *chasseurs à cheval* (light cavalry) provided reconnaissance for the army corps and participated in charges and the pursuit of the enemy. Left: a gunner on horseback from the Third Regiment wearing the dolman jacket of the full dress uniform.

Godoy, who was the lover of Queen María-Louisa. The king's staff despised Godoy and plotted to oust the ménage à trois and install Ferdinand, the eldest prince. In early 1808 Carlos arrested his son, then set him free. These schisms in the Madrid court led Paris to view Spain as a weak link in France's continental policy. Like their revolutionary predecessors, Napoléon and his circle did not trust their neighbor, which had lost its power and grandeur. Spain became a satellite and a backup force for France's plans. Following Talleyrand's advice, Napoléon offered to mediate the Spanish royalty's conflict. The intervention would be simple, he believed, as French troops were already in northern Spain as a rear guard of an expeditionary corps on its way to Portugal. Napoléon envisioned placing one of his own in Madrid, as Louis XIV had done a century earlier. For the first time since 1800, he yielded to pure ambition and the desire to conquer.

The success of the continental embargo on British goods depended upon French control of all European ports. Portugal, however, remained allied with England and ignored Napoléon's Berlin Decree of 1806, which established the blockade. The French crossed over Spain to punish Portugal's reigning House of Braganza (opposite, top). Lisbon fell on November 30, 1807, and the regent João VI went into exile. Napoléon's troops remained stationed in northern Spain, ready to seize control of that country at the first sign.

"The wretched war in Spain was a veritable scourge, the first cause of France's troubles."

On March 18, 1808, supporters of Ferdinand instigated the riots of Aranjuez and Carlos IV abdicated in favor of his son. A few days later, however, when troops led by General Murat under Napoléon's orders entered the Spanish capital, the king reneged upon his decision. It was an unmitigated imbroglio. The emperor invited all the actors to meet with him in Bayonne. There he elicited the abdication of both father and son. On May 9, 1808, he installed his brother Joseph Bonaparte (previously enthroned in Naples) in Madrid.

The announcement of Joseph's arrival caused an insurrection throughout Spain, and its leaders turned to England. London sent an expeditionary corps. By sheer force Joseph made his way and entered the capital. But the following day it was learned that General Dupont, having accepted bribes from the Spanish army, had surrendered dishonorably to Spanish nationalists in Bailén. This French humiliation was celebrated throughout Europe—the Grande Armée was not invincible. What ensued on the peninsula was horrific—ambushes, massacres, villages burned to the ground. It was not long before Joseph's fragile throne was threatened, and he was forced to abandon the capital. Only Napoléon's military intervention could save the situation.

He reunited his allies in Erfurt, where a disappointing diplomatic meeting revealed that the Russian alliance was not as solid as he had believed. The emperor advanced south,

On May 2, a few days before the abdication of Spain's Carlos IV and Ferdinand VII (above), the people of Madrid rose up—a prelude to the war of independence that would engulf part of the Grande Armée. The Madrilenos massacred several hundred soldiers of Murat's occupying army before being subdued the following day with brutal force. Left: Goya's famous *Tres de Mayo*, depicting the execution of the Spanish opposition.

creating havoc all along the route. After his victory in Somosierra on November 30, 1808, he entered Madrid and marched toward the expeditionary English corps, which fled. In another few weeks Spain was pacified. But on January 1, 1809, the emperor received some very bad news: Vienna had rearmed. The possibility of being attacked from the rear by a new coalition could not be ignored. The Austrians had to be addressed. Napoléon left the command to Marshal Soult and returned to Paris. He had become embroiled in something that was beginning to destroy his life's work. For the next five years Spain would be an ulcerated wound in the flank of his empire.

While the French battled insurgents rising up throughout Spain, General Dupont's troops advanced toward Cadiz to extricate the remains of the French navy that had been defeated at the Battle of Trafalgar. Unnerved by the uprisings throughout Andalusia, Dupont abandoned the plan and retreated. Spanish troops barred his passage at Bailén. On July 19, 1808, he tried unsuccessfully to attack. Three days later he surrendered (below). For the first time, the Grande Armée was defeated, humiliatingly. A poorly prepared and failed attempt to conquer, the war in Spain

"Enough spilt blood!"

The French surrender at the Battle of Bailén roused the Austrian public, which then pushed its government to avenge Austria's humiliating loss to France in 1805. War broke out in April 1809, when Archduke Charles and his troops invaded Bavaria. The French counter-offensive was immediate. Although his troops were inexperienced (a good portion of the Grande Armée was fighting in Spain), Napoléon succeeded in driving back

shook the Napoleonic system. It would end in 1813 with the Battle of Vitoria, where the French were crushed by Wellington's troops. Top: map of military operations in Spain from 1808 to 1813.

the enemy effort. Of even greater importance, a succession of French victories—Abensburg (April 20), Landshut (April 21), Eckmühl (April 22), and Regensburg (April 23)—opened the route to Vienna,

The French took Zaragoza on February 21, 1809 (below), after a heroic defense and perhaps 50,000 deaths.

The disaster at Bailén was followed on August 30, 1808, by the surrender in Sintra of French general Junot to the English. Napoléon, commanding 200,000 men, intervened on the Iberian peninsula, retaking Madrid in November 1808. Depicted here is the surrender of the capital, which he would hand over to his brother Joseph. A humane man of abundant good will, Joseph was dubbed by one of his biographers "the philosopher king" and by another "the king despite himself." He tried to be a modern monarch and to reform Spain with Enlightenment ideals, claiming to work for the good of "his" people. Cut off from the populace, confronted by merciless guerrilla tactics, and facing down an English expeditionary corps, Joseph would never achieve his goals. The Bonaparte experience in Spain was a failure: At its conclusion, Ferdinand VII, restored to power, would lead his country toward political isolation, repression, and a rejection of progress.

which Napoléon reoccupied on May 13, 1809.
Archduke Charles elected to withdraw, placing
the Danube River between him and the
French.

In the weeks that followed the adversaries
kept watch on one another. Napoléon's first
attempt to forge the river failed, resulting in
the bloody Battle of Essling (May 22). The
emperor decided to wait until June, when
reinforcements would arrive. His second attack
resulted in a difficult but decisive success on
July 6, 1809, at the Battle of Wagram—
Napoléon's last great victory.

For the first time the conqueror let his
weariness show. He offered to negotiate an end
to the hostilities with his enemies. They agreed
to a cease-fire and on October 14, 1809, signed
the Treaty of Vienna.

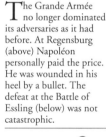

The Grande Armée
no longer dominated
its adversaries as it had
before. At Regensburg
(above) Napoléon
personally paid the price.
He was wounded in his
heel by a bullet. The
defeat at the Battle of
Essling (below) was not
catastrophic.

The first phase of the Napoleonic Wars culminated with a new victory for France. But cracks were beginning to appear in its structure. Spain continued to bleed. The Tyrol was rising up. German nationalism was gaining ground. The English desire to put an end to French power was as strong as ever. And although three years of relative peace followed and Napoléon's empire was at its apogee, there were signs presaging a fall.

At the Battle of Wagram, 190,000 of Napoléon's men and 140,000 of Archduke Charles's men faced off for two days. The decisive battle was launched from the French center following intensive artillery preparations with 100 cannons. Split in two, the Austrian army retreated without being pursued, as the French soldiers were exhausted.

These battle scenes illustrate the hardships the soldiers endured. Provisioning was exceptionally difficult—and usually done by pillaging (opposite, below). Caring for the wounded was another weak point of the Grande Armée, despite the dedication of individuals like Dominique-Jean Larrey, a military surgeon, and the organization of a health service. But war medicine was still rather rudimentary. A good number of the wounded would succumb in the weeks following a battle, after suffering atrocious agony. There were 6,000 French soldiers wounded at Austerlitz, 20,000 at Eylau and Wagram, 14,000 at Moskowa, 30,000 at Leipzig, and 20,000 at Waterloo.

A mere five years brought Napoléon from his apogee to his nadir. The imperial edifice that had appeared to be solid after Wagram began first to crack and then to implode under the pressure of foreign defeats, and the emperor did not move to halt his collapse in time. Europe had tired of this warmonger, this exporter of revolutionary principles, and was not inclined to accommodate him on the throne of a France it believed ought to reenter the fold.

CHAPTER FIVE
THE FALL
(1810–15)

"The vast edifice that he had created was exclusively of his own making and he alone was its keystone. The keystone was removed and the building collapsed from top to bottom."

Metternich,
Mémoires, 1880

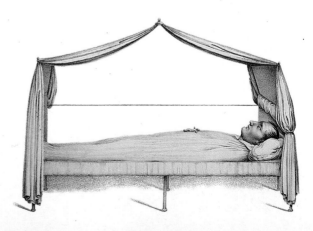

Napoléon disembarking at Saint Helena (left) and on his deathbed (right).

"One of my great ideas had been the conglomeration, the concentration of geographically like peoples who had been dissolved, fragmented by revolution and politics. I had wanted to make of each of these peoples a single, national entity."

In 1810 Europe was French. The system that Napoléon established comprised 130 departments (from Hamburg to Rome, Brest to Mayence) and the Kingdom of Italy, whose crown the emperor wore, with his stepson, Eugène de Beauharnais, serving as viceroy. Through a string of conquests, Napoléon placed members of his family on various thrones. His brother Jérôme ruled in Westphalia, while brother Joseph reigned first in Naples and then in Spain. Brother-in-law Murat was the grand duke of Berg, then king of Naples. Sister Elisa was the grand duchess of Tuscany. Brother Louis would remain the king of Holland until 1810, and his son Louis-Napoléon at age five reigned (through the intervention of French functionaries) over the grand duchy of Berg. The Bonaparte clan ruled French Europe, under the orders of Napoléon.

In addition, the emperor was the mediator of the Helvetic Confederation (Switzerland) and protector of the Confederation of the Rhine, which comprised sixteen minor German states. That alliance

The imperial court, its dignitaries, and its ponderous etiquette were introduced in 1804. Despite the appeal to some great nobles of the ancien régime, and notwithstanding the embroidery and the plumes, "these new debutants in the diplomatic service" (Mme. de Staël) would never quite forget they were upstarts. Below: Almost the entire imperial family (only Lucien, on poor terms with his brother, was absent) gathered for the marriage of Jérôme, named king of Westphalia four days earlier, to Catherine of Württemberg on August 22, 1807.

The years 1810–12 marked the apex of France's presence in Europe. The great empire extended beyond France's natural borders to include parts of Germany, Switzerland, Poland, and Italy, not to mention satellites governed by Napoléon's appointees. The son of the Revolution had wanted to bring the Enlightenment to oppressed peoples, but after 1807 his regime transformed into a machine of domination. Nationalistic sentiments germinated under French repression. Even after the French drew back, and despite Austria's and England's vigorous response, the vestiges and memories of the era would foster the birth of nations and the complete eradication, in less than a century, of the ancien régime.

with the kings of Saxony, Bavaria, and Denmark enabled him to tighten his grasp on Germany. Russia and Prussia had been his allies since 1807, and Austria had been brought to its knees in 1809. Only England, which supported the Spanish rebellion, remained at war with the Empire.

To fortify his Continental System, Napoléon developed lines of communication,

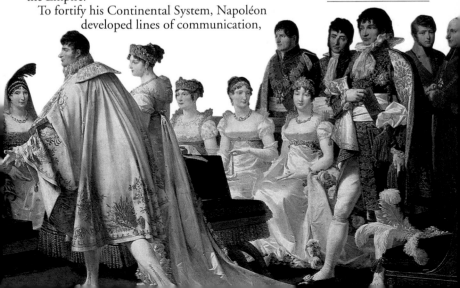

as well as cultural, legal, military, and economic exchanges with other countries on the continent. The Civil Code and a French-style administrative organization became law throughout Napoleonic Europe.

The flaw in this plan was that France ruled over the others, as Napoléon proved by annexing northern Germany, Holland, and Westphalia when their leaders undertook policies not to his liking. French Europe's vulnerability lay in its diversity, its immensity, and the coercion required to maintain it. In a backlash, European nationalist movements advanced their objectives on a wave of anti-French sentiments.

"I have decided upon the Austrian lady."

Another concern for the Empire at its height of power was that Napoléon had produced no direct heir to rule over the fourth dynasty. Joséphine could no longer have children and the emperor, assured of his fertility by the birth of his many bastards, was determined to renounce her. Their divorce was pronounced on December 14, 1809, and the annulment of the marriage by order of the Church of France was declared in January 1810.

Napoléon announced his decision to divorce Joséphine on November 30, 1809. The empress (she would retain her title) pretended to faint. She had feared this moment since the summer of 1800, when the idea of hereditary power for her husband was first mentioned.

It was a good time to make a new political marriage. After trying his luck with the czar to obtain the hand of his sister, Napoléon married Marie-Louise, archduchess of Austria. He thus became the nephew by marriage of Louis XVI. The civil marriage was celebrated on April 1, 1810, and the religious ceremony took place the following day.

"I marry a womb," the emperor declared to his entourage. On March 20, 1811, less than a year after their union, Marie-Louise gave birth to the long-awaited heir, who was immediately declared king of Rome. The hundred-cannon salute that greeted his birth also signaled the apogee of the Empire, which continued to enjoy relative peace on the foreign front.

When Francis I of Austria announced to his daughter, Archduchess Marie-Louise, that she was to marry the man she called "the Corsican," she was terrified. But the kindness of a Napoléon reinvigorated by the prospects of the union and by the birth of the king of Rome, successor of the fourth dynasty (below), would make this political marriage a private success until the final separation in 1814. Marie-Louise would remarry with Officer Niepperg. The king of Rome, recalled to Vienna, would die in 1832. Top: the marriage of Napoléon and Marie-Louise.

"The peace of the globe was in Russia, and success was by no means doubtful. I left."

After the Battle of Tilsit, Alexander I seemed to become a true friend of Napoléon. The romance would not last. Russia had revenge to take on Turkey, its traditional enemy, and would have been able to do so if its alliance with France had borne fruit. The idea was to share the spoils of the Ottoman Empire. Napoléon had promised to consider the matter. Turkey was already a "sick man," but France viewed it as a counterbalance in the event of a return to war with Russia and did not seek to hasten its disintegration. Another bone of contention was that Napoléon's creation of the grand duchy of Warsaw seemed to reconstitute Poland, Russia's enemy and the historical victim of its voracity. Finally, belonging to the Continental System had disrupted Russia's trade (while having stimulated the French and German economies)—although, with the czar's tacit approval, adherence to it

In spite of his "friendship" with the czar, Napoléon took steps that could only anger his ally, including his diplomatic relations with the Ottoman Empire, a historical enemy of Russia, and reinforcement of the grand duchy of Warsaw, created at Tilsit and enlarged after the defeat of Austria. Above: Napoléon receiving the ambassador of the Ottoman Empire on May 28, 1807; below right: Napoléon decorating Polish parliamentarians.

had slackened. In December 1810 the Russian government decided to tax imports from France. Other thorns in Franco-Russian relations were Alexander's snub when Napoléon asked for his sister's hand and the czar's displeasure when the emperor turned instead to Austria for a bride. A mere spark was all that was needed to touch off an explosion between Paris and Saint Petersburg.

Czar Alexander found his pretext when Napoléon annexed the duchy of Oldenburg in northern Germany, with the idea of tightening his hold on that part of Europe. Making matters worse, the sovereign of that minuscule state was Alexander's relative. By the middle of 1811 war was inevitable. It was delayed, however, as the czar wanted to make certain that Austria and Prussia, which had treaties with France, would not side with Napoléon. The Russian envoys verified that, while Vienna and Berlin were not yet prepared to join the fight against Napoléon, they did not want to place their armies at his disposal. Alexander also obtained an assurance of neutrality from the new royal prince of Sweden, the French marshal Bernadotte. Lastly, Russia signed a treaty with Turkey, which freed the southern flank from any immediate concern. The great confrontation could take place.

Czar Alexander I (1777–1825) was a young, indecisive sovereign who admired Napoléon and initially sought sweeping reforms. Then he was won over by mysticism and promoted a defensive policy based narrowly upon Russian interests, rejecting the Enlightenment and advocating reactionary policies.

"I think in three months it will all be over."

Napoléon did not sit passively by during the czar's political maneuvering. Rather, he forged the most extraordinary army of all time, amassing contingents from all over Europe. This "Army of Twenty Nations" comprised French, Italian, Spanish, German, Dutch, Austrian, and Prussian troops, among others. More than 500,000 men marched toward

the eastern borders of the empire. On April 8, 1812, Russia demanded France withdraw its troops and sign a trade agreement. On June 22, the Grande Armée crossed the Niemen River.

From the start, Napoléon did not consider seeking peace with Moscow. His objective was to force the Russians to attack the grand duchy of Warsaw so he could take them from behind in a turning movement. But the czar's army did not fall into the trap. Aware of its weaker numbers, it retreated from all fronts, forcing the Grande Armée to continue to advance, overstretching its lines. First the French took Vilna, then Vitebsk, then Smolensk, without fighting any decisive battles.

Kutusov, head of the Russian army, had adopted the systematic retreat and scorched-earth tactics of his

General Louis-François Lejeune painted many works detailing the particulars of battle. Above, his scene of Moscow. At the left, Eugène de Beauharnais and his white horse are impassive in the middle of a group of infantrymen while Murat, on the hill above, calmly gives orders to his staff officer. In the center, a gentlemanly Marshal Berthier lays down his sword. General Caulaincourt dies in the foreground.

predecessors. Then, allowing himself to be swayed by the czar's advisors, he agreed to battle in defense of Moscow. On September 7, 1812, the Battle of Moskowa (also known as the Battle of Borodino) took place 75 miles from Moscow. The two sides eviscerated each other. Napoléon, wanting to conserve his forces for another battle at Moscow, refused to supply reinforcements, leaving his regiments to fight to the finish. With nightfall Kutusov retreated, evacuating without fighting over Russia's historic capital. On September 14, in the company of 1,000 troops, Napoléon set out to occupy Moscow. At the instigation of Moscow's Governor Rostopchin, the Russians set fire to the city, leaving only smoldering ruins for the Grande Armée. Napoléon received no peace offering from the Kremlin.

After losing several weeks to waiting, the emperor left Moscow to tighten his lines and regroup his forces to the west. Winter arrived early, and the reserves of both food and

While the Russians were responsible for the burning of Moscow (above), Napoléon, who insisted upon waiting in the Russian capital for peace, made errors that certainly contributed to the catastrophe that began with this episode.

Scenes of the retreat from Russia: a grenadier before Cossacks harassing the columns (left). Napoléon and Murat warm themselves by a fire (near right). At Berezina, one of the last battles, the army crosses the river over bridges constructed by General Eblé's pontoniers (above). At that point, the Grande Armée was nothing more than a horde of stragglers (far right).

equipment were dwindling. On November 27, 1812, in a final effort, the Grande Armée managed to cross the Berezina River. After that point, it was an absolute rout. The army was ragged, scattered, and harassed by Cossacks. That was all that remained of the Army of Twenty Nations.

On December 5 the emperor abandoned his soldiers, returning to Paris to prepare for the next stage of the war. He entrusted the command to Murat, who likewise fled his post, returning to "his" Kingdom of Naples. At the close of 1812, only 20,000 men had crossed back over the Niemen River. The rest had either died, been taken prisoner, deserted, or, like the Austrian and Prussian divisions, returned to their own countries.

"On December 5, while proceeding on the route, we saw it covered with superior officers from different corps, as well as with the noble remains of the [Imperial Guard], covered in appalling furs and burnt overcoats, and others who had not even half of that. A great many walked leaning upon a pine branch; they were bearded and their hair was covered in ice. One saw those unable to walk looking amongst the wretched who covered the route, to find there the regiments they had commanded some fifteen days earlier, in hopes of obtaining help. He who had not the power to walk was a lost man. There were camps like bivouacs, resembling battlefields with so many corpses."

Memoirs of Sergeant Bourgogne

"I believe that nature has planned great reversals of fortune for me."

Upon returning to Paris on December 18, 1812, the emperor recognized his dynasty's fragile state. No one thought to proclaim his arrival. Just two months earlier, General Malet had succeeded in seizing some power for a

Leaving Moscow on October 18, 1812, Napoléon wanted to withdraw by a different route than the one he had taken to enter. But General Kutusov blocked his passage, forcing him to follow the route devastated during the march to the capital a few weeks earlier. The winter spared no one, including the emperor. The army's situation disintegrated rapidly: Regiments became disorganized, the spoils pillaged from Moscow slowed their progress, Cossacks massacred the laggards, the Russian army maneuvered to surround the remains of the Grande Armée, and desertions burgeoned (50,000 Frenchmen would remain in Russia). After the Battle of Berezina the collapse was complete. Napoléon relinquished command to Murat, who also abandoned it. At that point, there was no one left to command. More than 150,000 people were taken prisoner in the Russian campaign, and approximately 240,000 lives—two-thirds of them French—were lost to combat, sickness, hunger, and cold.

day, simply by announcing Napoléon's death, before the authorities regained their wits. News of the disasters in Russia, candidly reported (for the first time) in the official *Bulletin de la Grande Armée,* shocked the public.

Spurred on by the emperor's defeat and the devastation of his army, other nations began mobilizing. The English spread out over Spain, while the Russians pursued their advance. Austria and Prussia pondered when to rejoin the coalition.

In February 1813 the new coalition's bent became clear. The king of Prussia called for the mobilization of all of Germany against the French. Many duchies and principalities joined him in an alliance with England and Russia. Thus Napoléon would have to fight on two fronts: Spain and Germany.

The German campaign began in May. With approximately 3,000 men Napoléon fought the Russo-Prussian forces in Lutzen, Bautzen, and Wurschen. France's enemy withdrew. An armistice was signed (June 4) and a conference was convened in Prague. Then Austria decided to enter the war, and Bernadotte (the French marshal and heir to the Swedish throne) brought Sweden into the coalition.

In mid-August military operations resumed. Napoléon was victorious in Dresden but weakened by his marshals' defeats. He took on a decisive battle in Leipzig. This was a frontal assault in which the French were outnumbered two to one. The confrontation lasted three days

Facing down the European coalition in Germany, Napoléon was always victorious when he personally was in command. His discouraged lieutenants never reinforced his successes and, worse, suffered heavy defeats: Marshal Oudinot at Gross Beeren (August 23, 1813), Marshal MacDonald at Katzbach (August 26), General Vandamme at Kulm (August 30), where he surrendered with his corps of 30,000 men (left), and Marshal Ney at Dennewitz (September 6). Below: In Spain, Joseph Bonaparte was vanquished at Vitoria (June 21).

(October 16–19, 1813) before Napoléon ordered a retreat. Following a victory at Hanau, he recrossed the Rhine (November 2). France had already lost Spain after a disastrous defeat in Vitoria (June 21, 1813) and the widespread retreat of the emperor's lieutenants. In Naples, Murat—marshal of the Empire and king by his brother-in-law's mere will—negotiated the retention of his throne in exchange for a declaration of war against France. French forces surrendered throughout Holland and Belgium. France had returned to its state of 1792.

"Sixty thousand men and me—that makes one hundred and sixty thousand."

Napoléon turned down the draconian peace offers presented at the coalition's Frankfurt conference and energetically formed a small army. He believed France would be able to

The allied sovereigns give thanks after their victory at Leipzig (above). After his German allies joined the sixth coalition (England, Russia, Prussia, Austria, and Sweden), a betrayed Napoléon had to yield to the greater numbers.

regain the fervor of its revolutionary wars—without taking into consideration that it was his rigidity that had led the country toward ruin. He thus lost his final opportunity to save his throne.

At the beginning of 1814, when 250,000 allied forces united to the east of France, the odds were not on the French. On February 1 they were defeated on their own soil at La Rothière. But the allies made the mistake of dividing up their forces. Napoléon decided to defeat them one after another. In a brilliant defensive campaign, he did just that at Champaubert, Montmirail, Château-Thierry, Vauchamp, and Montereau. Overcome by this turn of events, but anxious to regroup their forces and finally to adopt a good war plan, the allies proposed a meeting at Chaumont. Fighting continued during the negotiations. Napoléon was victorious at Craonne and Reims but defeated in Arcis-sur-Aube. The allies intercepted couriers, revealing Napoléon's plans to take them from behind. Without waiting, they marched on Paris, refusing to fight.

On March 31, 1814, the allies entered Paris, which had been abandoned by Marie-Louise and Joseph Bonaparte, who was in charge of its defense. Napoléon installed himself at the Château de Fontainebleau, defended by Marshal Marmont's corps and his Imperial Guard. Little by little, his fate was sealed. The allies leaned to a return of the Bourbon monarchs, although the czar may have wanted to avoid that solution. In the capital Talleyrand played his own card, setting up a provisional government. On April 2 and 3, first the Senate and then the Legislative Body voted to dethrone Napoléon.

The emperor continued to plan for an attack, but his marshals, weary and demoralized, asked him to abdicate in favor of his son. On the night of April 4, 1814, Marmont's corps defected to the enemy with their weapons and kits. On April 6 Napoléon unconditionally abdicated, and the Senate called for Louis XVIII to ascend the throne. The allies accorded the ex-emperor sovereignty over Elba, an island in the Mediterranean

Wearing "his boots of 93," Napoléon once again became General Bonaparte during the French campaign. Leading 60,000 young recruits (nicknamed the "Marie-Louise"), he achieved a victory every two days. His troops were reinforced by survivors of the two preceding campaigns (opposite: the Imperial Guard) and supported by some of the peoples of the east who had organized into armed bands. Below: He is depicted followed by Marshals Ney and Berthier and Generals Drouot, Gourgaud, and de Flahaut.

ACTE D'ABDICATION

DE

L'EMPEREUR NAPOLÉON.

between Corsica and the Italian mainland. After crossing through a Rhône valley and a Provence hostile toward him, Napoléon set sail. On May 3 the brother of Louis XVI was returned to Paris.

Les Puissances alliées ayant proclamé que l'Empereur Napoléon était le seul obstacle au rétablissement de la Paix en Europe, l'Empereur Napoléon, fidèle à son serment, déclare qu'il renonce, pour lui et ses héritiers, aux Trónes de France et d'Italie

April 20, 1814, set the scene for the famous *Adieux de Fontainebleau* (opposite, below). With great emotion Napoléon addressed his Old Guard, kissed the flag of the First Regiment of Grenadiers, and departed on the road to exile. (Opposite: extract from the Abdication Act.) The victors granted him sovereignty over the island of Elba. He who had reigned over Europe now ruled a kingdom of 85 square miles and a population of 12,000. Left: Napoléon in the garden of his Portoferaio residence on Elba.

"I have renounced the idea of a great empire. Henceforth, the good fortune and the consolidation of the French Empire shall be the object of all my thoughts."

Europe had not seen the end of Napoléon, however. In less than a year's time he would be reinstalled at the Tuileries Palace (March 20, 1815) and Louis XVIII would again be an exile. In the meanwhile, it

must have been the people's disenchantment with the Restoration, the king's disinclination to pay the pension promised his predecessor, and the boredom gnawing at Bonaparte that gave rise to Bonaparte's envisioned return. On March 1, 1815, he landed at Cannes and, without a shot being fired, he and several hundred soldiers reconquered his empire.

A short while later Napoléon asserted that he was finished with undermining peace in Europe. He had returned with the intention of preserving the status quo born of his French campaign the previous year. But the nations that had united at the Congress of Vienna

On March 1, 1815, Napoléon landed in Cannes (above), which Chateaubriand described as the "invasion of a country by a single man." As "king of the island of Elba" he had promised in his first proclamation that the Eagle would fly "from belfry to belfry to the towers of Notre Dame."

(1814–15) to reestablish a balance of power in Europe made clear that they did not want a "Buonaparte" in Paris. On March 13, 1815, they pronounced him an "enemy and a disturber of the tranquility of the world." War was to resume. The emperor was the first to strike, his objective being to destroy the British army and the Prussians stationed in Belgium.

On June 12, 1815, Napoléon joined his 130,000 troops for a final campaign. On June 16 he was victorious in Ligny. Two days later, on the morning of June 18, the Battle of Waterloo began. The outcome was uncertain until the end of the day, when the Prussians, under Field Marshal von Blücher, burst onto the battlefield. Victory was theirs. They crushed the French, who were driven out despite the legendary resistance of the last division of Imperial Guard grenadiers.

After a hundred days in power Napoléon was forced to submit his second abdication on June 22, 1815. The consequences of his defeat this time were even more severe for France. Louis XVIII had been restored to power through a maneuver by Fouché. Severed from its territories, occupied by the enemy, ransomed by the allies, the country would no doubt have preferred to have forgone the Hundred Days adventure.

The Congress of Vienna (below), where Talleyrand represented Louis XVIII's France, banished Napoléon from Europe.

Napoléon's military epic ended on June 18, 1815, on the "dreary plains" south of Brussels. Anticipating an enemy movement toward France, he swept down upon Blücher's Prussian troops, which he defeated at Ligny. He then attacked Wellington's English army, which was entrenched near Waterloo. Some 74,000 French troops confronted 68,000 English troops. Despite his superior numbers, Napoléon lacked the resilience to win the fight. His lieutenants compounded his errors: Soult was a very mediocre major general; Ney annihilated the cavalry in senseless advances (top left); and Grouchy, whose 30,000 men had pursued the retreating Prussians, did not march toward the battlefield. The English resisted every inch of the way but were at the breaking point when Blücher burst upon the French right flank, provoking a chaotic retreat. Then "the Guard died, but did not surrender." Below left: the English at the Château d'Hougoumont.

"If Christ had not died on the cross, he would not be God."

Defeated, Napoléon surrendered to the English on July 14, 1815. Twenty-six years after the official start of the Revolution, London hoped to put an end to the great European convulsion by seizing the one who had always considered himself its rightful heir.

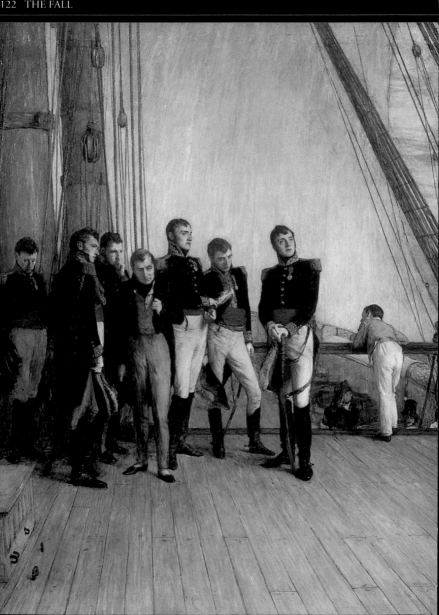

"Your Royal Highness, Exposed to factions that divide my country and to the enmity of the greatest powers of Europe, I have ended my political career and, like Themistocles, present myself at the hearth of the British people. I place myself under the protection of their laws and of this, Your Royal Highness, as the most powerful, the most determined, and the most generous of my enemies, I beg you."

Napoléon
Letter to the prince regent of England,
July 15, 1815

England did not accord its hospitality to the conquered. In agreement with the other members of the coalition, she booked him a prisoner's departure. He boarded the *Bellerophon* (left) for a voyage that would take him to the middle of the South Atlantic. In his school notebook the young Buonaparte had once written, "Saint Helena, little island."

To avoid the risk of a second return, the victors decided to exile the "Usurper" to Saint Helena, an island in the middle of the South Atlantic that had been a possession of the British Crown since 1659. In so doing, they presented him with the most honorable end to his career possible.

The place was an island "[chosen] by the devil flying from one world to the other," said Fanny Bertrand, wife

On Saint Helena Napoléon was consigned to the Longwood estate, where he could roam freely without an English escort. This view (above) was executed by his manservant Marchand.

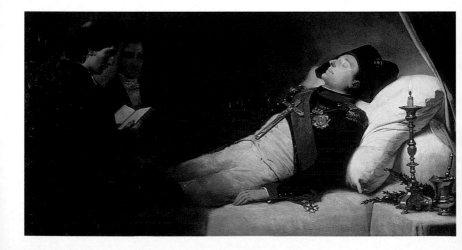

The deposed emperor divided his time between dictation to his companions in exile, tending and replanting his gardens at Longwood, the occasional stroll, and long conversations with anyone eager to listen and transcribe his words. Here he is depicted working with his companion Gourgaud. The final weeks of his life were especially difficult and painful. He suffered from cancer of the stomach, as had others in his family. After many days of agony, Napoléon

of one the emperor's last companions. Accompanied by a small, loyal circle, Napoléon survived five and a half years there in material wealth and promiscuity, both of which would divide his followers in petty jealousies. He would suffer as much from boredom as from the detestable climate and the harassment of his jailor-governor, Hudson Lowe.

While he rehashed his memories, he who once ruled the world occasionally devoted himself to gardening on his small estate of a few hectares—closely guarded by English sentries. But above all Napoléon wove his myth, dictating to his companions Las Cases, Gourgaud, Bertrand, and Montholon his version of the epic, in which the effigy of an uncompromising liberal succumbed to the blows of a conservative Europe. He died on May 5, 1821. As Chateaubriand would write, he was "the most powerful breath of life that ever animated human clay."

succumbed on May 5, 1821, at 5:49 in the evening (opposite).

"The initial fury passed, people of thought and judgment will bring me back."

The France of Louis XVIII began raising itself up from Napoléon's final failures, although the post-Waterloo period saw the occupation of the country by enemy troops. The Congress of Vienna had decreed an end to French influence over Europe, and for the next half century the victors would erect a "quarantine

In May 1840 Adolphe Thiers, a politician and Napoléon historian, announced to the chambers that King Louis-Philippe had obtained from England the right to return the emperor's body. On July 7 an expedition commanded by the prince of Joinville left Toulon for the voyage to Saint Helena. The ship lay anchor on October 8. On October 15 Napoléon's body was exhumed. On October 18 his ashes were transported to the frigate *La Belle Poule* (left), which then headed for France.

line" (R. Dufraisse) around the former Napoleonic Empire. The left bank of the Rhine was lost; the northern border was opened to every invasion. Within the country, the population recovered from the Revolution and the Empire, and various enterprises regained their strength. The "black legend" of Napoléon was at its height. The Ogre was attacked in violent pamphlets, as much by the liberals as by the royalists.

But this dark opinion did not have roots among a public formed by the Revolution and galvanized by the Napoleonic era. They nursed a diffuse nostalgia and rejected everything about the Restoration, notwithstanding the king's abilities. Forgiving what Napoléon had made them suffer during the final years of his reign, they rejected the "Ancien Régime in pants" (J. Jourquin) and began to turn toward its opposite.

ws cendres reposent sur les bords

au milieu Deupeuple

jai tout aime

Napoleon

On November 30, 1840, Napoléon's ashes arrived in Cherbourg. They continued on to

Beneath this stormy sky exploded a bombshell: the publication in 1823 of *Mémorial de Sainte-Hélène*, by Emmanuel de Las Cases, a companion of the exiled emperor until November 1816. Napoléon's exodus to Saint Helena and his solitary end in the middle of the ocean certainly struck people's sentiments. Las Cases presented the nation with both an authorized account of the "persecutions" the emperor endured and a reexamination of his accomplishments. The book's success was immediate and enormous. The "white legend" took flight, assuring the emperor's lasting triumph.

Le Havre, finally reaching Paris on December 15. Accompanied by vast throngs, the emperor traveled from the port of Courbevoie through the Arc de Triomphe and the Place de la Concorde to Les Invalides. He was laid to rest, as he would have wanted, by the banks of the Seine, among the French people.

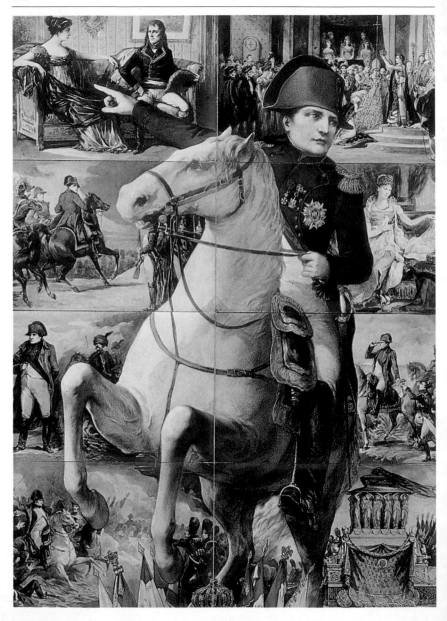

DOCUMENTS

NAPOLÉON Ier

Empereur des Français, Roi d'Italie, Protecteur de la Confédération du Rhin
& Médiateur de la Confédération Suisse

Love letters to Joséphine

"What is your strange power, incomparable Joséphine?" The man who ruled the world truly loved only one woman, she who accompanied him from the outset of the Napoleonic legend to the apogee of the Empire. The conqueror's love letters burst with his melancholy.

Paris, December 1795

I awaken filled with you. Your portrait and the intoxicating memories of last night have allowed my senses not the slightest rest. Sweet, inimitable Joséphine, what strange effect you have on my heart! Are you angry? Do I see you sad? Are you troubled? My soul is broken by pain and my love for you precludes rest…. But how could I rest anymore when, submitting to my deep-most feelings, I draw from your lips, from your heart, a flame that sets me alight? Oh, it is this night that instructs me how your portrait is not you! You leave at noon, in three hours I shall see you. Until then, *mio dolce amor*, a thousand kisses, but send none in return, for they would set my blood afire.

Albenga (Italy), April 1796

I received a letter that you interrupted, you said, to go to the country; and after that, you give the impression that you are jealous of me who is here, overwhelmed by work and exhaustion. Oh, my dear love!…I am not happy. Your last letter was cold, unfriendly. I could not find within it the fire that illuminates your eyes and which I had thought I sometimes had seen there….The fear of not being loved by Joséphine, the idea of seeing her capricious, of…. But I contrive worries. There are so many real ones! Is it necessary to create more!! You could not have inspired in me a limitless love, one unshared…. A kiss lower, lower than your breast.

Albenga, April 1796

Soul of my existence, write to me, with every post. I could not live any other way…. Farewell, farewell, farewell. I shall go to sleep, as sleep

Joséphine de Beauharnais in 1793.

brings me comfort. It sets you beside me; I take you in my embrace; but alas, upon awakening, sadly I find myself far from you.

Geneva, May 1800

I am in Geneva, my dear love. I shall be leaving tonight. I received your letter of the 27th.… I love you very much.… I should like you to write to me often and that you be convinced that my Joséphine is dear to me. A thousand happy thoughts to my little cousin. Tell him to be very wise. Are you listening?

Boulogne, August 1804

Madame and dear wife, your letter has found me in Boulogne. Tomorrow I shall be in Saint-Omer.… My health is good. I am working hard. But I am too wise. This is not good for me. It keeps me from seeing you and I send you a thousand happy thoughts.

Brünn, December 1805

Grand Empress, no letter from you since you left for Strasbourg. You traveled through Bade, Stuttgart, and Munich without writing a word to me. This is not nice, nor very tender!… Deign, from the heights of your grandeur, to concern yourself a little with your slaves.

Warsaw, January 1807

My love … the tone of your letters brings me despair, as does all that comes back to me. I forbid you to cry, to be distressed and troubled. I want you always to be gay, kind, and happy.

Paris, December 1809

My love, I find you today weaker than you should be. You have shown

courage, you must muster up some to sustain yourself; you cannot allow yourself to fall into a dire melancholy, you must be happy and, above all, take care of your health, which is so precious to me. If you have feelings for me, if you love me, then you must carry yourself with strength and make yourself happy. You must never place in doubt my constant and tender friendship.… Farewell, my love, sleep well. Dream the dreams I should for you.

Fontainebleau, April 1814

I shall, in my retirement, exchange the sword for the pen.…They have betrayed me, yes, everyone. I subtract from their numbers the good Eugène, as dignified as you and I…. Farewell my dear Joséphine, resign yourself just as I do and never lose the memory of the one who has never forgotten you and never will forget you.

C. de Tournier-Bonazzi,
Napoléon. Love Letters to Joséphine,
1981

Boulogne, August 1804.

Dictations from Saint Helena

The written output from Saint Helena was colossal, from Las Cases's Mémorial *to historical commentaries to eyewitness accounts. The fallen emperor recounted his memories and shaped his reputation for posterity. Here are some freely chosen excerpts.*

Battles

My battles cannot be judged independently. They had neither unity of place, action, nor intention. They were always a part of an extremely vast arrangement.

Emmanuel de Las Cases,
Mémorial de Sainte-Hélène, 1823

MÉMORIAL

DE

SAINTE-HÉLÈNE,

OU

JOURNAL OÙ SE TROUVE CONSIGNÉ, JOUR PAR JOUR, CE QU'A DIT ET FAIT NAPOLÉON DURANT DIX-HUIT MOIS;

PAR LE COMTE DE LAS CASES.

TOME PREMIER.

PARIS.

L'AUTEUR, RUE DU BAC, Nº 59;
TOUS LES LIBRAIRES DE FRANCE ET DE L'ÉTRANGER.

1823.

Brumaire

[When an] anticipated savior all of a sudden shows a sign of existence, the national instinct senses it and calls upon him; obstacles vanish in front of him, and the great masses, following at his heels, seem to say, "there he is!"

"Histoires du 18 brumaire," in
Correspondance de Napoléon 1er, 1870

Corsica

Never did the Romans buy Corsican slaves. They knew that one could extract nothing from them. It was impossible to mold them into servitude.
Mémorial de Sainte-Hélène

Government

To intend to rule over a people in an instant would be an act of madness. The genius of the worker must be to know to use the materials at hand. The secret of the legislator must be to know to take advantage of even the shortcomings of those whom he claims to govern.
Mémorial de Sainte-Hélène

Statesman

The man made for public life and authority sees not the individual; he sees only things, their weight, and their consequences.
Mémorial de Sainte-Hélène

France

The French nation is easier to govern when one does not go against the grain; nothing equals her ready and easy comprehension; she instantly distinguishes between those who work for her and those against her. But one must also always talk to her senses, if not, her anxious mind will gnaw at her and become agitated and angry.

Charles de Montholon,
History of the Captivity of Napoléon at Saint Helena, 1847

French Passion

The French people have two equally powerful passions that seem contrary, but which derive from the same sentiments—love of equality and love of distinctions. A government can satisfy these two needs only through extreme justness. The laws and the actions of the government must be the same for all; honors and rewards are bestowed on those men who are deemed most worthy. One pardons the deserving, not the schemer.

History of the Captivity

The French

It is merely that French people are lured by the prospect of danger. It seems to give them spirit; it is their Gallic heritage … valor, love of glory are instinctive to the French, a sort of sixth sense.

Mémorial de Sainte-Hélène

The Republic

The republic is the organization that rears the best soul and which possesses to the greatest degree the seed of great things; but its grandeur will sooner or later devour it because, to be powerful, an absolute necessity is a unity of action, which leads to despotism by a man or the aristocracy.

History of the Captivity

The Revolution

The Revolution was the rising up of the whole nation against another part of the nation; that of the third estate against the nobility, the reaction of the Gauls against the Francs.

Mémorial de Sainte-Hélène

Robespierre

If he had not succumbed, he would have been the most extraordinary man ever to have existed…. I regret not having known him.

General Bertrand,
Notebooks from Saint Helena, 1949–59

Waterloo

A singular victory where, despite the most horrible catastrophe, the glory of the vanquished did not suffer, and that of the victor did not swell. Memories of the former will survive its demise; memories of the latter will perhaps be buried in its triumph.

Mémorial de Sainte-Hélène

General Bertrand weeping beside Napoléon's body, May 5, 1821.

Napoléon viewed by his contemporaries

After the fall of the Empire, participants in the regime published their memoirs. Profiles of Napoléon by his contemporaries were innumerable. Both first- and third-person accounts presented him as a statesman, often as a superman, and sometimes as a very short man. Perhaps within this wealth of perspectives resides the character's human "truth."

Following Las Cases's *Mémorial* (1823) and the memoirs (1822) of Barry Edward O'Meara (a physician who attended the exiled emperor), some of Bonaparte's other companions on Saint Helena produced their own work. However, those books, including Antomarchi's (1825) and Montholon's (1847), never rivaled their predecessors. A continuous wave of publications, varying in quality and accuracy, drew hordes of readers:

memoirs by Fouché (1824), Savary (1828), Bourrienne (1829), and the valet Constant (1830–31); memoirs by military heads such as Rapp (1823) and Gouvion Saint-Cyr (1831); dramatic and puerile accounts by soldiers in Napoléon's old guard, including Coignet (1851) and Bourgogne (1898); and those by such brilliant cavalrymen as Parquin (1845) and Marbot (1891).

At the Brienne military college

We were just eight years old, Napoléon and I, when our relationship began; it would soon become quite close. There was between us one of those sympathies of the heart that announces itself quite quickly. I was continually delighted by this friendship, this intimacy that lasted from childhood until 1784, when he left the military college at Brienne for the one in Paris....

I have read, "As a student, he was solitary at school; as a schoolmate, he had no equals. He had friends who were subservient." There is no truth in this.... In the seven years that I was his schoolmate, I never saw anything that would justify this deplorable word play.

At Brienne Bonaparte was known for the color of his skin, which the

The good emperor.

French climate had greatly changed, for his piercing and inquisitive look, and for the tone of his conversation with his masters and schoolmates. There was almost always a harshness in his comments. He was very rarely friendly. I believe this must be attributed to the misfortunes that befell his family at the time of his birth and the impressions the conquest of his country made upon him in his first years....

In general, Bonaparte was not well liked by his schoolmates, who certainly were not subservient. He spent little time with them and rarely partook in their games…. As soon as it was time for recreation, he ran off to the library, where he would avidly read historical books, above all by Polybus and Plutarch…. The young Corsican's character became even more bitter by the mocking of the students, who often made fun of his name Napoléon and his country. He said to me many times, with humor, I will do to your French as much harm as I can…. Although Bonaparte rarely had praise for his schoolmates, he disdained registering complaints about them, and when he had surveillance duty imposed on him, he preferred to go to prison than to denounce petty infractions….

Memoirs of Monsieur de Bourrienne on Napoléon, the Directory, the Consulate, the Empire and the Restoration, 1829

The Great Man as seen by his valet

Upon his return from Egypt, the Emperor was extremely thin and very yellow, his skin color copperish, his eyes rather dark, his physique perfect, although a bit thin. His forehead was very high and open. He did not have much hair, especially at the temples, but it was very fine and soft. It was a chestnut color and his eyes were a beautiful blue, and they depicted in an incredible manner the different emotions that stirred him—at times extremely tender and gentle, at other times severe and even coarse. His mouth was beautiful, the lips equal and a bit tight, particularly when he was in a bad mood. His teeth, while not very regular and straight, were very white and very good. He never complained about them. His nose, Greek in form, was faultless, and his sense of smell was extremely keen. In short, the whole of his face was uniformly handsome…. His neck was a little short, his shoulders rounded, his chest large and very slightly hairy, his thighs and legs shapely; his feet were small, the toes straight and utterly devoid of corns and calluses; his arms were well formed and hung well; his hands were admirable, and the nails did not spoil them; additionally, he always took the greatest care of them, as he did his whole person, but without affectation.

Memoirs of Constant, First Valet to the Emperor, on the Private Life of Napoléon, His Family and His Court, 1830–31

Nothing but a man

(This scene took place during a military review at the Tuileries Palace.) At one o'clock, a grand drum roll, whose echo thundered off the sides of the château, announced the Emperor. His white horse awaited him at the bottom of the stairs to the château.

He jumped somewhat heavily upon him and took off at a canter, followed by the prince de Neuchâtel, Marshal Bessière, the duke de Feltre, and a dozen generals.

After stopping for some fifteen minutes at the right wing of the Portuguese grenadiers, where he asked questions I could not understand, he inspected all the lines and returned to place his feet on the ground where he had mounted his horse....

Here, I must mention one thing hardly royal, hardly imperial, that took place before our eyes, even before the eyes of the women packed into Marshal Duroc's apartments. Bonaparte felt the need and, unceremoniously, he relieved himself in the corner of the entry door. Of this I say no more. Following this gallant episode, I watched as His Majesty nonchalantly walked toward us, down the length of the château wall, scratching his navel and taking snuff.... That day, as almost every other, he wore the uniform of his guard. Two rather measly colonel's epaulettes and the little cross were his only marks of distinction. A small black hat adorned with nothing more than a cocarde the size of an ecu, a strong, plain sword, white jacket and britches, heavy boots, this was his outfit.

An easy bearing, but one without an air of nobility, a natural way and a total absence of a sense of propriety characterized Napoléon that day. I do not know if he took it upon himself to appear hard and crude because he was commanding his soldiers and had intentionally borrowed the noble profession's manners and energetic language. Half-seated upon a rock, he in due time had his right hand in his britches, and in due time again his arms and legs were crossed. Constantly he took snuff, quickly taking a pinch in a single jerk of his right hand.... The facial expression of the Emperor would change in accordance with the mood of the moment. I have seen it in two extremes. That day it bespoke great severity and contempt.

Colonel de Luternan, "Paris en 1810," *Revue de Paris*, August 1950

Poorly raised, but very brilliant

Above all, it was during the four years of Bonaparte's Consulate that one could study this extraordinary character. During this period, he was accessible to everyone. He presented himself exposed; he invited almost every person who visited to his table; and as he very much liked to chat, there were very few important questions upon which one had not heard him debate and expound. He even invited his ministers and foreigners dressed in tails and boots. Quite often one would spend the entire day with him at his country house in Malmaison, taking walks, playing games, and conversing.

Bonaparte was truly great and respected. The memory of his victories, the comparison between the state of anarchy just recently ended with the new order of things, and a veritable freedom won him the hearts of all.... Bonaparte was held in high esteem and respected outside the country. And if he had known to limit his ambitions there, he would still be on the French throne, surrounded by the blessings of the public. But Providence decided otherwise.

People who were rarely near Napoléon, or those who only saw him for a few moments, could only judge him rather unfavorably. His first impression was cold and his remarks insignificant or dishonest. He was not in possession of those proprieties that a worldly upbringing and proper education give…. One cannot deny, however, that Napoléon was quite spirited and piquant in conversation, but it was only in discussions that he developed those qualities. He was very eloquent, even, when he was animated and when he wanted his opinion to prevail. I have heard him make many remarks that would make the fortune of a man of intellect.

My Memories of Napoléon by Count Chaptal, 1893

In his private offices

I have already stated that the Emperor did not receive visitors in his inner cabinet; he went into the adjoining sitting room to work with those who asked for him. There, two small tables covered with green cloth bordered by a gold fringe were placed diagonally before the two corners at the back of the room. Each table held a writing case, and behind them was an armchair reserved for the Emperor. When he sat at one table or the other, he turned his back on the rear of the room and had the window in front of him. The minister spread out the papers from his portfolio on the edge of the cloth and only sat down himself when the Emperor, seeing a change to be made, a development to be added, or some instruction to give for a new task, got up and dictated his ideas. The minister then placed himself at the end of the table, taking notes and retaining as best he could all that the Emperor was dictating…. Sometimes Napoléon summoned a secretary to write, and the other vacant table served this purpose.

Ordinarily the meeting took place standing: the Emperor walked back and forth across the room to the window and the person speaking to him followed the same movements.

Napoleon: How He Did It: The Memoirs of Baron Fain, 1909

The good emperor

Before leaving France, he terminated all those affairs that could not be resolved in his absence. Such had been his habit each time he went on a journey; normally, he would take each minister aside to give him specific instructions, if he wanted to do something that ought not become the subject of a correspondence. He was meticulous regarding every small detail; he deemed nothing beneath his dignity to attend to; and when in the final week of his stay, he would address all the business that remained with his ministers. He referred to this as cleaning his office, because he found solutions to many of the problems that he had been addressing for a long time and remained unanswered.

Upon his departure, he informed me of everything he wanted me to do during his absence; these were general instructions that he gave me and which were far from being as strict as supposed by those men who spent their lives painting [Napoléon] as a tyrant who possessed neither justice nor goodness in his heart. These were precisely the two qualities he had in abundance. He had infinite pleasure regarding that which provided him an opportunity to do somebody justice, and one need not fear to ask such of him, as he never declined to proffer it.

I should not, however, want to deny that there were many acts undertaken by his administration that persecuted individuals and were even ruinous for some families. There is almost none amongst them that I could not justify, as all the caustic measures that he took during certain circumstances had been solicited in advance in official reports addressed to him....

In the instructions that the Emperor gave me prior to his departure, he did not cease to instruct me not to be severe and to manage everyone carefully. He made note that one never gains anything by creating enemies and that, especially with the Ministry of Police, a light touch was obligatory. He told me ten times that no one was to be arrested arbitrarily and to take great care always to have reason on my side.

Savary, *Memoirs of the Duke of Rovigo*, 1828

Courageous and near the soldiers

Many people depict Napoléon as a violent, hardened, and short-tempered man. These are people who have never been near him. Undoubtedly, absorbed as he was by his work, vexing in his views, constrained in his projects, he was impatient and uneven in his temper. Nevertheless, he was so good, so generous that he often had to be calmed down....There are those who claim that Napoléon was never brave. A man who, having started as a simple artillery lieutenant and became the head of a nation such as ours could not be in want of the least bit of courage.... He knew how he had enemies among the Jacobins and the *chouans;* nevertheless, almost every evening he went out and walked through the streets, mixing into the crowds, never accompanied by more than two people.

During the 1806 campaign

Napoléon arrived at camp and reviewed the Third Corps.... The generals, the officers, the noncommissioned officers were called around his person. "I wanted to gather you," he said to them, "to declare to you the great satisfaction that the fine conduct you displayed in battle has inspired in me.... I have lost some brave ones; they were my children, I miss them. But in the end, they died on the field of honor, they died as true soldiers! You have paid me a great service in this memorable circumstance. It is above all owing to the brilliant conduct of the Third Corps that we have obtained such brilliant results. Tell your soldiers that I am satisfied with their courage...." Monsieur Denon was present at this emotional scene; perhaps his paintbrush will consecrate the memory; but whatever his talent, he will never paint the air of satisfaction and the kindness that spread over the sovereign's features, nor the devotion, the recognition upon everyone's faces.... The proclamation that Napoléon addressed to the troops filled them with new fervor.

During the Russian retreat, the emperor came to realize that he was once again without the rear guard under the command of Marshal Ney.

Napoléon walked at the head of his guard and spoke often of Ney. He recalled his accurate and swift glance, his courage in the face of every ordeal, ultimately everything that made him so brilliant on the battlefield. "He is lost. Alas! I have 300 million at the Tuileries, I would give it if he were brought back to me." He set up his headquarters at Dubrovna. We resided at the home of a Russian lady who had been courageous enough not to abandon her house. I was on service that day; the Emperor summoned me to him at about one o'clock in the morning. He was very downtrodden. It would have been difficult for him not to have been so, the picture as horrible as it was….We left for Orsza and resided with the Jesuits. Napoléon was despairing over seeing the rear guard again…. The next day we pushed on through two places; we were stopped in an awful hamlet. It was the Emperor who, toward evening, learned of the arrival of Ney and his joining with the Fourth Corps. One can easily imagine the joy he felt and the welcome he gave the marshal the following day.

Memoirs of General Rapp,
aide-de-camp of Napoléon,
written by himself, 1895

The last day

May 5, day of the emperor's death

From midnight to one o'clock, constant hiccups, but much worse. From one o'clock to three o'clock, he drank more frequently. He first raised his hand, then turned his head to drink no more. At three o'clock, very severe hiccups; moaning that seemed to come from far off.

From three o'clock to four-thirty, some hiccups, silent groans after the moaning, he yawns; it appears he suffers greatly; he said a few words that could be heard, and "who retreats," and certainly, "At the head of the army."

From four-thirty to five o'clock, great weakness, groans. The doctor raised his pillow up a little. The Emperor no longer opens his eyes. He appears weaker than at dawn. He is no more than a corpse. His undershirt covered with red spittle that has not the strength to run further. The curtains have been opened….

Until ten-thirty, eleven o'clock, generally calm; respiration light; the body perfectly motionless; a few movements of the pupils, but rarely; the eyes fixed, hooded, are three-quarters closed. From half-hour to half-hour, a few sighs and sounds. A second tear in the same place; the right hand on top of the bedclothes; the left hand on his thigh. Since six o'clock, very calm, motionless.

Sixteen people present, twelve of whom are French…. At seven-thirty, he is poorly. From eleven to noon, [Doctor] Arnott placed mustard plaster on his feet and [Doctor] Antomarchi two vesicatories, one on his chest, the second on his calf. The Emperor let out a few sighs. Several times, the doctor checked the pulse at the neck.

At two-thirty, Doctor Arnott placed a bottle filled with boiling water on his stomach.

At five-thirty, the Emperor let out his final sigh. The three last minutes, he let out three sighs….

At the moment of the attack, light movement of his pupils, regular movement of his mouth and chin together; as regular as a pendulum. At night, the Emperor pronounced the name of his son before saying, "at the head of the army." At dawn, he had asked two times, "What is my son's name?" Marchand answered, "Napoléon."

Général Bertrand,
The Notebooks of Saint Helena,
January–May 1821

Napoléon's triumph

While Napoléon's epoch was the 19th century, reminders of the emperor are still quite present today, notwithstanding an indifference toward his educational and university systems. From bureaucratic institutions to European nationalism, from the myth to the political heritage, from Romanticism to the names of streets, he is everywhere. Chateaubriand got it right when he wrote, "Alive, he lost the world. Dead, he owns it."

Napoléon's century

With the fall of his empire, Napoléon's myth took flight. It flourished during the Romantic period, culminating with the return of Napoléon's ashes in 1840. It was through Napoléon's adventures that the Romantics sought to cure their "century's sickness." Born under his regime, cradled by his glory (the writers Dumas and Hugo were both sons of generals), they could no longer take part in it. They would discover in a new form of literature the "battlefield" that they lacked, attribute to the emperor objectives he did not have (the defense of freedom, for example), and make him the champion of their quest for energy and the absolute.

In the years after 1815, Casimir Delavigne's *Les Messéniennes* ignored the disaster and sang the final act of

L'*Apothéose de Napoléon* (*Apotheosis of Napoléon*), watercolored lithograph by Jean-Baptiste Isabey, after a painting by Horace Vernet.

the epic. Abroad, Esaias Tegnér (*The Eagle's Nest*) and Heinrich Heine (*The Two Grenadiers*) followed at his heels. Upon Napoléon's death, the eruption of popular works surged, among them *The Fifth of May* by Pierre-Jean de Béranger and Alexander Pushkin's *Ode to Napoléon*. Then came Victor Hugo (*Ode to the Napoléon Column*), August Barthélemy and Méry (*Son of the Man* and *Waterloo*), Alexandre Dumas (*Napoléon or Thirty Years in History*), and many others.

The imperial epic, fed by the accounts and memoirs of players in the regime that multiplied over the century, became the backdrop for Romantic literature. The Napoléon of the people came to life through the works of Béranger (*Memories of the People* and dozens of popular songs), Charles Augustin Sainte-Beuve (*Volupté*), Alfred de Vigny (*Grandeur and Military Service*), Gérard de Nerval (*Napoléon and France at War*), Alfred de Musset (*Confession of a Child of the Century*), Edgar Quinet (*Napoléon*), and above all, Balzac (*The Country Doctor, The Gondreville Mystery, The Bureaucrats, A Woman of Thirty, Colonel Chabert*, etc.) and Stendhal (*The Red and the Black, The Charterhouse of Parma*). Philosophers furthered the cause: Hegel saw in Napoléon the "soul of the world." In time all artistic disciplines followed suit. In music there was Berlioz and Beethoven; in painting, Vernet, Charlet, Delacroix, Géricault, Ingres, et al.; and in sculpture, Seurre and Rude.

Before the 19th century came to an end, every great French author would write about Napoléon. Such a plethora of novels, poems, odes, and memoirs could not but infiltrate French society and bolster the nostalgia for a glorified, bygone past.

Chateaubriand: The black legend

Every nation has its vices. Those of the French are neither treason, nor darkness, nor ingratitude. The murder of the duke of Enghien…, the war in Spain, and the arrest of the Pope revealed something in Napoléon foreign to French nature.… The time will come, I hope, when free Frenchmen will, in a solemn act, declare that they took no part in these crimes of tyranny, that the murder of the duke of Enghien, the arrest of the Pope, and the war in Spain were impious, sacrilegious, odious, and above all, anti-French acts, the shame of which must only fall upon the head of foreigners.

Chateaubriand,
Of Buonaparte and the Bourbons, 1814

Byron: The victor overthrown

'Tis done—but yesterday a King!
  And arm'd with Kings to strive—
And now thou art a nameless thing:
  So abject—yet alive!
Is this the man of thousand thrones,
Who strew'd our earth with hostile bones,
  And can he thus survive?
Since he, miscall'd the Morning Star,
Nor man nor fiend hath fallen so
    far.…

The Desolator desolate!
  The Victor overthrown!
The Arbiter of others' fate
  A Suppliant for his own!
Is it some yet imperial hope
That with such change can calmly cope?
  Or dread of death alone?
To die a prince—or live a slave—
Thy choice is most ignobly brave!…

Thine evil deeds are writ in gore,
  Nor written thus in vain—

VIVANDIÈRE DE L'ARMÉE

Thy triumphs tell of fame no more,
    Or deepen every stain:
If thou hadst died as honour dies,
    Some new Napoleon might arise,
    To shame the world again—
But who would soar the solar height,
To set in such a starless night?…

There was a day—there was an hour,
    While earth was Gaul's—Gaul thine—
When that immeasurable power
    Unsated to resign
Had been an act of purer fame
Than gathers round Marengo's name,
    And gilded thy decline,
Through the long twilight of all time,
Despite some passing clouds of
    crime.…

But thou forsooth must be a king,
    And don the purple vest,
As if that foolish robe could wring
    Remembrance from thy breast.
Where is that faded garment? where
The gewgaws thou wert found to wear,
    The star, the string, the crest?
Vain froward child of empire! say,
Are all thy playthings snatched away?
                        Lord Byron,
    "Ode to Napoleon Buonaparte," 1814

Balzac: A Napoléon soldier on watch

"Tell us about the Emperor!" cried
several voices at once.

"You will have it?" answered
Goguelat. "Very good, but you will see
that there is no sense in the story when
it is gone through at a gallop. I would
rather tell you all about a single battle.
Shall it be Champ-Aubert, where we
ran out of cartridges, and furbished
them just the same with the bayonet?"

"No, the Emperor! the Emperor!"

The old infantry man got up from
his truss of hay and glanced round
about on those assembled, with the
peculiar sombre expression in which
may be read all the miseries, adventures,
and hardships of an old soldier's career
[followed by Goguelat's recap of the
Napoleon campaign; the epic tale ends
in Waterloo]. France is prostrate, the
soldier counts for nothing, they rob him
of his due, send him about his business,
and fill his place with nobles who could
not walk, they were so old, so that it
made you sorry to see them. They seize
Napoleon by treachery, the English shut
him up on a desert island in the ocean,
on a rock ten thousand feet above the
rest of the world. That is the final end
of it; there he has to stop.… A lot of
them say that he is dead! Dead? Oh! yes,
very likely. They do not know him, that
is plain! They go on telling that fib to
deceive the people, and to keep things
quiet for their tumble-down government. Listen; this is the whole truth of
the matter. His friends have left him
alone in the desert to fulfill a prophecy
that was made about him, for I forgot
to tell you that his name Napoleon
really means the LION OF THE
DESERT. And that is gospel truth. You
will hear plenty of other things said
about the Emperor, but they are all

A soldier from Napoléon's old guard (above), sketch by Huart for an illustration for *The Human Comedy*. Right: Stendhal's typographic experiments for the cover of his *Vie de Napoléon* (*Life of Napoléon*).

monstrous nonsense. Because, look you, to no man of woman born would God have given the power to write his name in red, as he did, across the earth, where he will be remembered for ever! . . . Long live 'Napoleon, the father of the soldier, the father of the people!'"

Honoré de Balzac,
The Country Doctor, 1833

Stendhal: "He was the greatest."

Napoléon's truest glory was to remake the spirit of the French people. He was the greatest man to have appeared in the world since Caesar. He was our only religion....

We were later unfaithful to this religion, but in all the important matters, just as the Catholic religion does for its faithful, it regained a hold on our hearts.

Today, in 1837, the peasants and the

MEMOIRES

SUR

V̶IE

D̶E̶ NAPOLÉON

lower classes in all the civilized countries of Europe have almost understood that the French Revolution led to making them property owners, and it is Napoléon who gave them this education.

Stendhal, *Life of Napoléon,* 1837

Hugo: The Colossus on the column

Sire, to thy capital thou shalt come back,
　　Without the battle's tocsin and wild stir;
Beneath the arch, drawn by eight steeds coal black,
　　Dressed like an emperor.

Thro' this same portal, God accompanying,
　　Sire, thou shalt come upon the car of state;
Like Charlemagne, a high ensainted king,
　　Like Caesar, wondrous great....

An acclamation, tender, lofty, sweet,
　　A heart-song high as ecstasy can bear it,
Shall fill, O captain mine! the city's street,
　　But thou shalt never hear it....

The baptism of the king of Rome. "The future! The future! The future is mine!"

While round thy form gigantic, like a
        friend,
    France and the world awake in
        shadows deep,
Here in thy Paris ever, world without
        end,
    Thou shalt lie fast asleep;…

Like to those soldiers marching bolt
        upright
    So often after thee to field or
        town,
Who by the wind of battle touch'd one
        night
    Suddenly laid them down;…

Yea, so much like, that seeing thee
        all ice,
    Like a mute god permitting
        adoration,

They who came smiling, love-drunk,
        in a trice
    Shall raise a lamentation.…

Yea, thou shalt be to all a presence
        solemn,
    Both good and great,—to France an
        exile high
And calm; a brass Colossus on thy
        column
    To every stranger's eye.…

The while thy name without a peer
        shall soar,
    Illustrious, beautiful to Heav'n, ah!
        thou
Shalt in the darkness feel for evermore
    The grave-worm on thy brow.
                        Victor Hugo,
            "The Emperor's Return," 1840

"The only recompense for genius is immortality and glory": Napoléon and the 20th Century

Theater (Edmond Rostand, G. B. Shaw), philosophy (Friedrich Nietzsche), and literature (Camille Claudel, Anatole France, Léon Bloy, André Suarès, Elie Faure, Charles Maurras, Louis Aragon, André Malraux, and more recently Patrick Rambaud, Jean-Paul Kauffmann, Max Gallo, et al.) continue to draw inspiration from the character of Napoléon.

Certainly film has seized onto the epic and its heroes. In 1897 the Lumière brothers produced their *Meeting Between Napoléon and the Pope,* beginning an uninterrupted series of films on the subject, the most recent of which is Yves Angelo's *Le Colonel Chabert* (1994), the most renowned, Abel Gance's *Napoléon* (1927).

Barrès: Professor of energy

Professor of energy, such was his definitive physiognomy and his decisive formula, obtained by the superimposition of all the images of him—by specialists, artists, and ordinary people—that we recall. From so many Napoléons, the shared traits represented to us an exciter of the soul. When the years will have destroyed the works of this great man, when his genius is no longer considered of use by thinkers and ordinary people, when all the conditions of social and individual life that he had envisioned will have been changed, something will, however, endure: his power to multiply energy. May the elite of humanity, using it according to its needs, recognize it and honor it as such. There is a striking saying in Russia, "There is no man as powerful as he to whom the czar speaks, and his power lasts as long as the words that he hears." Even when the words of Napoléon are no more, when they cease to be something positive, when his code, his principles of war, his authoritarian system will have lost their vitality, one of his virtues will continue to come forth and extricate individuals and peoples of good sense who at times sense death and raise them up at the right moment so as not to fear the absurd.

Maurice Barrès, *The Uprooted,* 1897

"The face of God in the shadows"

Napoléon's history is certainly the least well known of all histories. The books that pretend to relate it are innumerable and documents of all kinds go on ad infinitum. In truth, Napoléon is less known to us than Alexander [the Great] and Sennacherib [the Assyrian king]. The more one studies, the more one discovers that he is the man who resembles no one, and that is it. Here is the chasm. One knows the dates, one knows the deeds, the victories and the disasters, one knows something or much of the famous negotiations, which today are nothing more than dust. Only his name remains, his prodigious name, and when it is pronounced even by the poorest of all children, anyone would blush, for he was a great man. Napoléon, it is the face of God in the shadows.

It is well known that prophecies and biblical foreshadowings could not have been understood until after they were fully realized; that is to say, when what was hidden will have been revealed.... Napoléon was inexplicable, and without a doubt the most inexplicable of men, because he was, first and foremost, the harbinger of He who must come and who perhaps is not far off; a harbinger

Napoléon by Abel Gance, a masterpiece of Napoleonic cinema.

and precursor very close to us, himself informed by all the extraordinary men who had preceded him throughout the ages. If one chooses to accept this postulate and probes it a bit, the History will take on a completely new aspect and the Napoleonic ocean, so terribly tumultuous until now, will all at once become calm beneath a sky of miraculous serenity.

Léon Bloy, *The Soul of Napoléon*, 1912

The sublime monster

September 7, 1812. Dreadful word from Napoléon to Murat the evening of the Battle of Moskowa. This battle was the bloodiest of all wars prior to 1914. There were ninety thousand men killed or wounded, sixty thousand were Russians, thirty thousand French. The horrid stench and the groans, the death rattles and the dust rising up from this carnage; and the setting sun illuminating it. For the French side as much as the Russian, the disaster was appalling. Across an expanse of a square league, as stated by General Rossetti, "the ground was covered with the dead and the wounded." Heaps of corpses. A hell of pain. The wretched wounded, piled up one upon the other, deprived of aid and swimming in their own blood, let out horrible groans and, in great cries, begged for death. The emperor observed the battlefield and said, "I would not have believed it SO BEAUTIFUL."

Here are the words that paint the monster in all his grandeur. Sublime, when a matter of himself and his mission, horrific when a matter of his victims. A monster is not merely the head of Medusa with its snakes for hair, nor the Hydra with its hundred heads—it is the prodigy, the strange form that nature creates just once. In such a monster, the tremendous and the fearsome are always present. Overwhelming and ghastly, the monster was a spectacle. He walked over the vastest cemetery the world had seen since Tamerlan. He stopped; grew tired on foot. The lugubrious evening exited from the ground; it did not fall from the sky, which drew it up. The horrid purple mounted from the hundred thousand agonies—thirty or forty thousand Frenchmen amongst them, who that morning were filled with future days, with joys, with youth and strength, who had, there in the sweet land to the West, mothers and sons and wives. And the monster felt joy in his heart there before his work. It was a good job and he admired it as a connoisseur....

What really could be the humanity of a Napoléon? The order that he established and the obedience he demanded. His humanity was the administration, as his destiny was politics. Such is the monster of power. And all-powerful ones, in the order of the flesh, strive after this monster, but they do not all have the genius. All the absolute rulers, all the conquerors, whether they be from Assyria or Rome, or Arabia, from Faustin I of Haiti to Caesar, they are a rough sketch of Napoléon.

André Suarès, *Views on Napoléon*, 1933

Malraux and De Gaulle: Conversation on Napoléon

On the cover of ... a weekly, there was a large portrait of Napoleon.

"What do you think of the Emperor?" the General asked me.

"A very great mind, and a rather small soul."

"But that wouldn't have been the right thing to say in Corsica...."

I was to have spoken at Ajaccio to commemorate the Emperor's birth, and at the Invalides, the General was to mark the return of his ashes to Paris.

"It seems to me," I said, "that he never faced metaphysical or, if you prefer, religious questions. Read the *Mémorial.* We always hear about his superstitions—as if so many of the greatest religious minds were not superstitious! But his religion, his real religion, must have been fairly akin to his mother's. Great conquerors rarely ask themselves the meaning of life...."

The General answered, with the half-smile that seemed to mean one more encounter with human oddity, "He had not time for the soul. Consider, at Saint Helena.... When did he make the remark I have quoted, 'Yes, it is sad; like greatness...'?"

"When he came back to the Tuileries, after Elba."

... "And then," he went on, "in an historic personality, the legendary creative power—you understand what I mean—takes the place of the soul."

"What would you have said, at the Invalides?"

"He left France smaller than he had found her, granted; but that is not what defines a nation. For France, he had to exist. It is a little like Versailles: it had to be done. Don't let's sell grandeur short."

André Malraux,
*Felled Oaks: Conversation
with De Gaulle*, 1971

Historiography

With tens of thousands of books devoted to him, Napoléon, along with Jesus Christ, is the historical figure most examined by historians and writers. But from this heap the emperor does not emerge as a single entity. To each his own Napoléon!

The truth is quite difficult for history to draw

From the historiographic point of view, the subject of Napoléon is infinite, a source of endless debate. It is through this continuous stream of works that historians sift, judge, study, and recount his fate. "The story of Napoléon must be rewritten every fifty years," wrote Stendhal. Indeed, an endless army of writers has done so, each binding the emperor within his own truth.

So who was Napoléon? No one can say. There are as many Napoléons as there are testimonials, historians, and citizens. Although the Napoleonic episode was a brief moment in European history—concluded, theoretically, on the "dreary plains" of Waterloo—it has never ceased to affect the collective memory.

A man of order

Napoléon possessed titles that we must neither ignore nor forget, and to which, in some corner of our birthright or our convictions or our interests, we are linked. Without question, in organizing our social state by the Civil Code, our administration by its regulations, he did not give us a political system under which our society would definitively stay tranquil and live peaceably, prosperous, and free; he did not give us freedom, which his heirs still owe us; but in the aftermath of the disturbance of the French Revolution, he could only procure for us order, and we must be grateful to him for having given order to our civil state and our administrative bureaucracy.

Adolphe Thiers,
History of the Consulate and the Empire, 1862

The founder of the bourgeois state

Napoléon could disappear—observe how his work responded more to his unalloyed ambition than to the needs of the nation, legitimatized once again as a great European empire. Under the veil of despotism, the essential institutions of a free state were in place, those that answered to the new economy and the modern bourgeoisie. The new dominant class, having first seized the power of the state in 1815, found that control continued to elude it, to the advantage of the personal dictatorship; it would not definitively regain control until 1830. Despite the events of the 19th century—the "revolution" of 1848, the coup d'état of 1852, the collapse of the Second Empire, the rise of the political bourgeoisie at the end of the century—the organs of the Napoleonic state remained in place. So do they continue today, notwithstanding the events of the 20th century—the collapse of the Third Republic in 1940 and the coup d'état in May 1958—demonstrating the solidity of the great Napoleonic opus.

Albert Soboul,
Civilization and Napoleonic France,
1983

Jean Tulard: The archetype of the saviour

Faced with internal or external threats to its interests, the French bourgeoisie has always been able to invent a saviour. Napoleon opened the way for Cavaignac, Louis-Napoleon Bonaparte, Thiers, Pétain, and de Gaulle. And because the bourgeois's principal virtue is ingratitude and its major defect lack of courage, the separation of the saviour from his inventors has more often than not come about through a national catastrophe. After a few years a suicidal tendency can be discerned in him, a tendency which was present even in de Gaulle, according to Malraux. Is he weary of power or disgusted by his role? The saviour appears out of tragic circumstances ..., he disappears in an apocalyptic atmosphere. Another saviour will take his place and the wheels will start rolling again. In all this can be seen the consequences of the disappearance of the principle of legitimacy on which the old monarchy was based before 1789.

Napoleon is the archetype for these saviours who are landmarks in the history of nineteenth- and twentieth-century France.

Jean Tulard, *Napoleon:
The Myth of the Saviour*, 1977

HISTOIRE

DE

L'EMPIRE

FAISANT SUITE

A L'HISTOIRE DU CONSULAT

PAR

M. A. THIERS

ÉDITION ILLUSTRÉE DE DEUX CENT QUATRE-VINGTS DESSINS

Chronology

1769

August 15: Birth of Napoleone Buonaparte in Ajaccio.

1779

May 15: Enters the military college in Brienne.

1784

October 22: Enters the military college in Paris.

1785

February 24: Death of Carlo Buonaparte, Napoléon's father.

September 28: Napoléon receives the rank of second lieutenant and joins the La Fère regiment (November 3).

1786

September 15: First of many leaves to Corsica. This one lasts a year.

1788

June 15: Stationed at Auxonne, Napoléon vacillates between allegiance to Corsica and France.

1789

April 1: Napoléon partakes in the repression of a riot at Seurre.

July 19: He helps quash another riot in Auxonne.

October 30: He departs for Corsica, where he is active in nationalistic clubs.

1790

Napoléon spends the year in Corsica, trying to ingratiate himself with

Paoli, the island's military governor, who has distanced himself from the Bonaparte family.

1791

Napoléon returns to France (February). At Jacobin meetings in Valence, he declares himself for the Republic. He returns to Corsica in the fall.

1792

Upon returning to France, Napoléon stays in Paris. He helps in the defense against the insurrections of June 20 and August 10 (the taking of the Tuileries Palace). His receives the commission of captain in July. He returns to Corsica in October.

1793

February 22: Napoléon receives his baptism by fire during the siege of the island of San Stefano (Sardinia), leading the Corsican voluntary forces.

March: Breaks with Paoli, as decreed by the Convention's indictment.

May: Following a brief trip to the continent, Napoléon returns to Corsica as part of the Republican Army, whose purpose is to suppress the revolt by Corsicans loyal to Paoli. The expedition will prove a failure, and the entire Bonaparte family will leave the island in June.

July 29: Publication of Napoléon's *Le Souper de Beaucaire* (*The Supper at Beaucaire*).

September 16: Napoléon is appointed commander of the artillery and takes part in the siege of Toulon. The city is dramatically retaken by the French (December 19).

December 22: Napoléon is promoted to brigadier general.

1794

February–July: Napoléon partakes in numerous military operations in northern Italy.

August 9: Napoléon is arrested as a supporter of Robespierre, who had been overthrown and executed in July. Ultimately he escapes the purge and saves his military career.

1795

June 13: Napoléon is assigned to the Army of the West.

October 5: He partakes in the events of 13 Vendémiaire, defending the Tuileries against a mob of royalists.

October 26: He is appointed commander-in-chief of the Army of the Interior.

1796

March 2: Napoléon is appointed commander-in-chief of the Army of Italy.

March 9: He marries Joséphine de Beauharnais.

April: Start of the Italian campaign. Victories in Montenotte (April 12), Millesimo (April 13), Dego

(April 15), Mondovi (April 21), Lodi (May 10), Lonato (August 3), Castiglione (August 5), Roveredo (September 4), Bassano (September 8), Saint Georges (September 15), and Arcole (November 15–17).

1797

January 14: Victory at Rivoli.

April 18: Peace negotiations with the Austrians in Leoben.

October 18: Treaty of Campoformio.

1798

April 12: Napoléon is appointed commander of the Orient.

May 19: Departs with the fleet to Egypt.

June 10: Occupation of Malta.

July 1: Disembarks near Alexandria; start of the Egyptian campaign. Victories at Chebreis (July 13) and the Pyramids (July 21).

July 25: Enters Cairo.

August 1: The English navy defeats the French at Aboukir.

October: Conquest of Upper Egypt by Desaix (through January). Revolt of Cairo (October 21).

1799

Syrian campaign: The taking of El-Alrich (February 20) and Jaffa (March 7). Defeat at Saint Jean d'Acre (March–April). Victory at Mount

Tabor (April 16). Evacuation from Syria.

August 22: Napoléon leaves for France.

October 13: Napoléon arrives in France.

November 9, 10, and 11: Coup d'état by Napoléon and Sieyès.

End of December: Adoption of a new consular constitution with three consuls: Napoléon (first consul), Cambacérès, and Lebrun.

1800

February 13: Creation of the Banque de France.

February 17: Law concerning the administrative organization of France.

May–June: Second Italian campaign. Victory at Marengo (June 14).

December 3: General Moreau victorious at Hohenlinden.

December 24: Assassination attempt on the first consul.

1801

February 9: Peace Treaty of Lunéville with Austria.

March 28: Peace Treaty of Florence with Naples.

July 15: Signing of the Concordat.

October 8: Peace Treaty of Paris with Russia.

1802

March 25: Peace Treaty of Amiens with England.

April 26: Amnesty for émigrés.

May 19: Creation of the Legion of Honor.

June 25: Peace with the Ottoman Empire.

August 2: Napoléon is declared consul for life.

1803

April 30: France cedes Louisiana to the United States.

May 16: Treaty of Amiens is broken; preparations for the invasion of England begin.

December 1: Institution of the workers' passbook.

Throughout the year numerous acts are passed regarding the organization of the notary and the minting of the "germinal" franc.

1804

February–March: The "great conspiracy" to overthrow Napoléon fails; its leaders are arrested and executed. Moreau is exiled. The duke of Enghien is executed by firing squad (March 20).

March 21: The Civil Code is put in force.

May 18: Proclamation of the Empire. Eighteen marshals are named the following day. Reestablishment of the court and of court etiquette.

July: Plebiscite on the question of hereditary succession to the throne.

December 2: Coronation of Napoléon.

1805

May 26: Napoléon is crowned king of Italy in Rome.

April–August: Russia, Austria, and Naples join forces with England against France.

October 14: French victory at Elchingen.

October 19: Austrian surrender at Ulm.

October 21: French naval disaster at Trafalgar.

November 14: Napoléon enters Vienna.

December 2: Victory at Austerlitz.

December 26: Peace Treaty of Pressburg with Austria.

1806

January 1: Reestablishment of the Gregorian calendar.

March 18: Establishment of labor conciliation boards.

March 30: Joseph Bonaparte becomes king of Naples.

May 10: Creation of the Université de France, which would become imperial in 1808.

June 5: Louis Bonaparte becomes king of Holland.

July 12: Creation of the Confederation of the Rhine, of which Napoléon is the protector.

July–October: Prussian campaign. Victories at Jena and Austerlitz (October 14). Occupation of Berlin (October 27).

November 26: The Berlin Decree establishes the Continental System (economic blockade).

1807

January–February: Polish campaign, which comes to an end with the butchery at Eylau (February 8).

June 14: Victory at Friedland.

June 25–July 9: Meeting at Tilsit between Napoléon and Czar Alexander I, who forge a peace.

August 18: Jérôme Bonaparte becomes king of Westphalia.

September 11: Publication of the Commercial Code.

September 16: Creation of the Revenue Court.

October–November: France's victorious campaign in Portugal, under Junot.

1808

February 2: Occupation of Rome.

March 1: Creation of the imperial nobility.

April–July: Intervention in Spanish affairs: Decree of Bayonne and the abdication of Carlos IV and his son Ferdinand; riots in Madrid upon the naming of Joseph Bonaparte to the Spanish throne. Defeat at Bailén (July 22).

November: Spanish campaign under Napoléon's command. Victory at Somosierra (November 30). Napoléon leaves Spain in mid-January 1809.

1809

March–April: Austria rearms. Napoléon enters Bavaria.

May 13: Taking of Vienna.

May 22: Battle of Essling.

July 5–6: Victory at Wagram. Austria proposes a cease-fire and signs a peace treaty in October.

July 7: Arrest of Pope Pius VII.

December 14: Napoléon divorces Joséphine.

1810

February 17: Rome reunited with the Empire.

March 3: Reestablishment of state prisons.

April 1: Marriage of Napoléon and Marie-Louise.

July 9: Annexation of Holland.

December 13: The senatus consultum divides imperial France into 130 departments.

1811

March 20: Birth of Napoléon's heir, the king of Rome.

June–December: Crisis within the Church of France following the failure of a national council and the refusal of the pope to enthrone new bishops.

1812

June–December: Russian campaign. Taking of Vilna (June 28) and Smolensk (August 17). Victory at Moskowa (September 7). Entry into Moscow (September 14). Beginning of the retreat (October 19). Crossing of the Berezina (November 25–28).

October 23: In Paris, General Malet's plot to seize power destabilizes the Empire.

December 5: Napoléon abandons his army.

December 18: Napoléon arrives in Paris.

1813

May–October: German campaign. Austria and Prussia align themselves with England, Sweden, and Russia. Napoléon is victorious at Lutzen (May 2), Bautzen (May 20), and Dresden (August 26–27). He is defeated at Leipzig (October 16–19).

1814

February 1: Defeat at Rothière.

February–March: Victories at Champaubert (February 10), Montmirail (February 11), Château-Thierry (February 12), Vauchamp (February 14), Montereau (February 18), and Craonne (March 7).

March 20: Defeat at Arcis-sur-Aube.

March 31: Allies enter Paris.

April 6: Napoléon abdicates.

April 20: *Adieux de Fontainebleau*; Napoléon departs for Elba.

1815

March 1: In a bid for reconquest, Napoléon disembarks at Cannes (Golfe de Juan).

March 20: He arrives at the Tuileries.

April 23: *Acte Additionel aux Constitutions de l'Empire*, which limited the emperor's powers and assured individual rights.

June 15: French enter Belgium.

June 16: Victory at Ligny.

June 18: Defeat at Waterloo.

July 15: Napoléon offers himself to the English.

October: Napoléon arrives at Saint Helena. He takes residence at Longwood December 10.

1821

May 5, 5:49 p.m.: Napoléon dies.

Filmography

Major films about the Napoleonic era or about Napoléon himself, based upon a filmography collated by Jean Tulard.

Napoléon, Gance, France, 1927.

The Firefly, Leonard, United States, 1937.
Conquest, Brown, United States, 1937.
Désirée, Koster, United States, 1954.
War and Peace, Vidor, United States, 1956.
The Pride and Passion, Kramer, United States, 1957.
Imperial Venus, Delannoy, France, 1962.
War and Peace, Bondarchuk, USSR, 1968.
Waterloo, Bondarchuk, USSR–Italy, 1970.

Love and Death, Allen, United States, 1974.
The Duellists, Scott, England, 1977.
Time Bandits, Gilliam, United States–England, 1982.
Le Colonel Chabert, Angelou, France, 1994.

Further Reading

Barzun, Jacques. *The Modern Researcher.* 5th ed. New York: Harcourt Brace Jovanovich, 1985.

Blaze, Elzéar. *Military Life under Napoleon, The Memoirs of Captain Elzéar Blaze.* Chicago: Emperor's Press, 1995.

Chandler, David G. *Dictionary of the Napoleonic Wars.* New York: Macmillan, 1979.

Cronin, Vincent. *Napoleon Bonaparte, An Intimate Biography.* Devon, England: Newton Abbot, 1971.

de Chair, Somerset, ed. *Napoleon's Memoirs.*

London: Soho Book Company, 1986.

Durant, Will and Ariel. *The Age of Napoleon.* New York: MJF Books, 1975.

Herold, J. Christopher, ed. and trans. *The Mind of Napoleon—A Selection from His Written and Spoken Words.* New York: Columbia University Press, 1955.

Marchand, Louis-Joseph. *In Napoleon's Shadow: Being the First English Language Edition of the Complete Memoirs of Louis-Joseph Marchand, Valet and Friend of the Emperor, 1811–1821.* San

Francisco: Proctor Jones Publishing, 1998.

Montholon, Charles-Tristan, comte de. *History of the Captivity of Napoleon at St. Helena by General Count Montholon.* Philadelphia: Carey and Hart, 1847.

Tulard, Jean. *Napoleon: The Myth of the Saviour.* Translated by Teresa Waugh. New York: Beaufort Books, 1984.

INTERNET SITES

www.napoleon.org (site of the Fondation Napoléon)

www.napoleonica.org (site

with documents and archives)

www.napoleonguide.com (useful site for preliminary familiarization and research)

www.napoleonseries.org (extensive site; entries of varied quality posted by professionals and amateur enthusiasts)

www.napoleonic-literature.com (literature of the Napoleonic age; links to full texts and bibliographies)

www.100megsfree4.com/ napwars (curios on the Napoleonic Wars, maps, book reviews)

List of Illustrations

Key: *a*=above, *b*=below, *l*=left, *r*=right, *c*=center

Front cover: Jacques-Louis David (1748–1825), *Le Premier consul franchissant le mont Saint-Bernard,* painting, Versailles.
Spine: First Consul Bonaparte, engraving, Bibliothèque Thiers.
Back cover: Sir W. Q. Orchardson, *Napoléon On Board the Bellerophon* (detail), painting, Tate Gallery Publications.
1 C. von Steuben (1788–1856), *Retour de l'île d'Elbe, mars 1815* (detail), Kunsthandel, London.
2 Vernet, *Napoléon passant devant les troupes à Iéna* (detail).
3 François Gérard (1770–1837), *Bataille d'Austerlitz* (detail), painting, Château de Versailles.

4 Auguste Couder (1789–1873), *Napoléon visitant l'escalier du Louvre* (detail), painting, Musée du Louvre, Paris.
5 Claude Gautherot (1769–1825), *Napoléon harangue le 2e corps de la Grande Armée, à Ausbourg, 1805* (detail), painting, Château de Versailles.
6 Jean-Louis Ernest Meissonier (1815–1891), *Campagne de France* (detail), painting, Musée d'Orsay, Paris.
7 Giuseppi Serangeli (1768–1852), *Napoléon et Alexandre I à Tilsit, le 9 juillet 1807* (detail), painting, Versailles.
8 Sir W. Q. Orchardson, *Napoléon On Board the Bellerophon* (detail), painting, Tate Gallery Publications.
9 Charles Meynier (1768–1832), *Napoléon dans l'île Lobau sur le Danube,*

after Essling (detail), painting, Versailles.
11 C. von Steuben, *Les Huit Époques de Napoléon,* painting.
12 Baron Gros (1771–1835), *Bonaparte au pont d'Arcole,* painting, Versailles.
13 Jean-Baptiste Greuze (1725–1805), *Bonaparte,* engraving, Malmaison and Bois-Préau.
14a Bonaparte at Brienne, engraving after the painting by Réalier-Dumas, Bibliothèque Thiers.
14b Christofle, Bonaparte at Brienne, bronze after Rochet, Malmaison and Bois-Préau.
15a French school, late 18th century, *Charles-Marie Bonaparte,* Musée de la Maison Bonaparte, Ajaccio.
15c Certificate of nobility presented in 1779 to Napoleone de Buonaparte,

archives, Ministère de la Guerre.
15b French school, 19th century, *Marie Laëtitia Bonaparte,* painting, Musée de la Maison Bonaparte.
16a P. Grégoire, Siege of Toulon, drawing, Bibliothèque Nationale de France (BNF), Paris.
16b *Dernière entrevue entre Bonaparte et Pascal Paoli en Corse,* painting, Musée départmental Pascal Paoli, Morosaglia (presently in the Musée Fesch).
17 Buonaparte, life drawing, Bibliothèque Thiers.
18a Raffet, *Le 13 Vendémiaire,* drawing.
18c P. Barras, engraving.
18–19 Baron Gros, *Joséphine,* painting, Malmaison and Bois-Préau.
19a Marriage of Bonaparte and Joséphine

de Beauharnais, 1796, engraving, BNF.

19c Marriage certificate of Bonaparte and Joséphine Tascher de La Pagerie, widow of General Beauharnais, March 9, 1796 (detail).

21a Map: First Italian campaign.

20–21b H. F. E. Philippoteaux, *Bonaparte à la bataille de Rivoli*, 1844, painting, Versailles.

22–23 Bacler d'Albe, *Bataille de pont d'Arcole*, painting, idem.

24–25 Giuseppi Pietro Bagetti (1764–1831), *Entrée des troupes françaises à Milan*, watercolor, idem.

26a J. Navlet (1821–1889), *Bonaparte donnant l'ordre de restaurer La Cène* (after Da Vinci), painting.

26b Bonaparte, general in command of the French Army of Italy, engraving, Bibliothèque Thiers.

27 Béranger, *Vase étrusque réprésentant l'arrivée au Louvre des objets d'art acquis par Napoléon lors de la campagne d'Italie* (detail), 19th century, painting on porcelain, manufactured by Sèvres, Musée de la Céramique, Sèvres.

28 Petition from Sheik Sulayman al-Fayoumi to General Bonaparte, 23 Frimaire Year VII, Musée de L'Emperi, Salon-de-Provence.

28–29b François-André Vincent (1746–1816), *Bataille des Pyramides*, painting, Château de Grosbois.

30a Baron Gros, *Les Pestiférés de Jaffa*, painting, Musée du Louvre.

30b Jean-Baptiste Isabey (1767–1855), Bonaparte in the uniform of the Institute of Egypt, miniature on ivory, private collection.

31 Jean-Léon Gérome

(1824–1904), *Bonaparte en Egypte*, painting, private collection.

32 Jean-Auguste-Dominique Ingres (1780–1867), *Bonaparte, premier consul*, painting, Musée des Beaux-Arts, Liège.

33 L. Meyer, *Arrivée de Bonaparte à Antibes, à son retour d'Egypte*, painting, Versailles.

34 François Bouchot, *Le 18 Brumaire*, painting, idem.

35a Duplessis-Bertaux, Emmanuel Sieyès, engraving, Marcel Robillard collection.

35b François-Xavier Fabre (1776–1837), *Lucien Bonaparte*, painting, Museo Napoleonico, Rome.

36 Chataignier, the three consuls, drawing and engraving, Bibliothèque Thiers.

37a Auguste Couder (1789–1873), *Installation du Conseil d'État le 25 décembre 1799*, painting, Versailles.

37b Jean-François Garneray (1755–1837), *Talleyrand*, Musée Lambinet, Versailles.

38 Charles Thevenin (1764–1838), *Passage du Grand Saint-Bernard le 20 mai 1800*, painting, Versailles.

39 Jacques-Louis David (1748–1825), *Le Premier consul franchissant le mont Saint-Bernard*, painting, idem.

40a Assassination attempt on the Rue Saint-Nicaise, engraving, Malmaison and Bois-Préau.

40–41b Bonnefoy, *La machine infernale*, engraving, Bibliothèque Thiers.

41a Pacification of the Vendée, Year VIII, engraving, BNF.

42a "Senatus consultum of 24 Thermidor Year X, holdings of the Senate."

42b First Consul Bonaparte, engraving, Bibliothèque Thiers.

43 Bonaparte and Joséphine at Malmaison, print, BNF.

44–45 Courvoisier Voisin (1757–1830), Malmaison, gouache, Malmaison and Bois-Préau.

45 J.- L. Vignes (1819–1879), *La Rose de Malmaison* (detail), painting, idem.

46a Polignac, *Mort de Cadoudal*, watercolor, Musée Carnavalet.

46b Martinet, judgment of the duke of Enghien, engraving, BNF.

47 Jean-Paul Laurens (1838–1921), *Mort du duc d'Enghien*, painting.

48 David, *Distribution des Aigles au Champ-de-Mars, 5 décembre 1804*, painting, Versailles.

49a Georges Rouget, *Napoléon reçoit, le 18 mai 1804, le sénatus-consulte qui le proclame Empereur des Français*, painting, idem.

49b David, emperor crowning himself, study, Musée du Louvre.

48–49b Martin-Guillaume Biennais (1764–1843), *Glaive de l'Empereur*, Musée Napoléon-Ier de Fontainebleau.

50–51 David, *Le Sacre de l'Empereur Napoléon Ier*, painting, Musée du Louvre.

52 Anne-Louis Girodet-Trioson, *Napoléon en costume de sacre*, painting, Musée de Montargis.

53 Order of the Legion of Honor decoration, Musée Napoléon-Ier de Fontainebleau.

54–55a Basset, a small family, drawing and

engraving, Bibliothèque Thiers.

55b The first consul visits the Sevene Brothers factory in Rouen, drawing with sepia wash, 1804, Versailles and Trianon.

56b With the overall peace, Napoléon resheaths his sword, engraving, BNF.

56–57a July 14 Year XI, fireworks after the Treaty of Lunéville, stamp, Musée Carnavalet.

57 Dominica Doncre, *La Paix d'Amiens*, painting, 1802, Musée des Beaux-Arts, Arras.

58a The great Napoléon reestablishes the rights of the Jews, May 30, 1806, engraving, Bibliothèque Thiers.

58b Baron François Gerard, signing of the Concordat July 15, 1801, bistre wash on paper, Versailles.

58–59 "Law of 18 Germinal Year X regarding Protestantism."

59 Engraving announcing an Easter Mass on April 18, 1802.

60a *Exposition des produits industriels dans le cour du Louvre en 1801*, watercolor, Musée Carnavalet.

60b Bertrand Poirot-Delpech, attire of the chief judge of the minister of justice, 1808, lithograph, Bibliothèque Thiers.

61a Student at the Lycée Napoléon, drawing.

61b Dress attire of the prefects, 1810, idem.

62 Idem, page 4.

63a Place du Carrousel, triumphal arch erected in Paris to the glory of the Grande Armée, after a drawing by Fontaine and Percier.

63b Étienne Bouchot, *Place du Châtelet: fontaine élevée en 1808 pour* *commémorer l'expédition d'Egypte*, painting, Musée Carnavalet.

64 Jean-Baptiste Debret (1768–1848), *Première distribution de la Légion d'honneur église des Invalides, 14 juillet 1804*, painting, Versailles.

65a Boily, *Cambacérès duc de Parme*, painting, BNF.

65b The emperor's copy of the Civil Code, private collection.

66l Dominic Bosio, *Galerie du Palais-Royal*, painting, Musée Marmottan, Paris.

66r Ecu worn by the great French dukes, BNF.

66–67a Benjamin Zix, *Cortège nuptial de Napoléon et Marie-Louise le 2 avril 1810*, Musée du Louvre.

67b Serangeli, *Napoléon reçoit, au Louvre, les députés de l'Armée après son couronnement*, painting, Versailles.

68a Worker's passbook instituted by the police in 1809, Archives de la Seine.

68b Robert Lefèvre (1755–1830), *Anne-Jean-Marie-René Savary duc de Rovigom ministre de la Police générale sous l'Empire*, painting, Versailles.

68–69a *Gazette de France*, April 23, 1806.

69l The Decree of Moscow regulating the Théâtre Français.

69r Edouard Louis Dubufe (1820–1883), *Josephe Fouché duc d'Otrante, en grand habit de ministre de la Police sous l'Empire*, painting, Versailles.

70 J. Marchand, Napoléon at the apogee of his glory, engraving after a painting by J. Chabord, Bibliothèque Thiers.

71 Napoléon's travel case. Musée Carnavalet.

72–73 Effects of the Continental System, French caricatures, BNF.

73b Gilleray, Gulliver and the king of Brobdingnag, June 26, 1803, caricature, private collection.

74–75a Jean-François Hue (1751–1823), *Napoléon au camp de Boulogne, juillet 1804*, painting, Versailles.

74–75b Idem, page 5.

76–77 Thevenin, *Reddition d'Ulm (20 Octobre 1805)*, painting, Versailles.

76b Proclamation of Austerlitz (detail).

77 Map: Campaigns of 1805, 1807, and 1809.

78–79 Idem, page 3.

80–81a French school, *L'Empereur poursuit les Russes après Friedland, juin 1807*, 19th century, sepia wash, Versailles.

80–81b Edouard Detaille (1848–1912), *Le Soir d'Iéna*, painting, Musée de l'Armée, Paris.

82–83 Charles Meynier, *Entrée de Napoléon dans Berlin le 27 octobre 1806*, painting, Versailles.

84–85 Meynier, *Napoléon visitant le champs de bataille au lendemain Eylau le 9 février 1807*, painting, Versailles.

86a *Maréchal Berthier*, painting, Musée de l'Armée.

86c Tito Marzocchi de Belluchi (1800–1871), *Maréchal Davout*, painting, Versailles.

86b Marshal Lannes, after Baron Gérard, Musée de l'Armée, watercolor, Versailles.

86–87a S. Fort, *Charge décisive de la cavalerie à Eylau*, watercolor, Versailles.

87b Detaille, *Napoléon et Murat avant Friedland*, watercolor, Bibliothèque Marmatton, Boulogne-Billancourt.

88al Officer of the *voltigeurs* Eight Infantry Regiment in the *Grande Armée 1807*, after a manuscript by Otto, Anne S. K. Brown Military College, John Hay Library, Brown University, Providence, Rhode Island.

88ar Foot grenadiers of the Imperial Guard, idem.

88bl Fireman of the Third Infantry Regiment, idem.

88br Officer of the 24th Regiment of the Cavalry, idem.

89 Artilleryman on horseback.

90–91b Francisco de Goya (1746–1828), *Los fusilamientos del tres de mayo*, painting, Muséo del Prado, Madrid.

91a Junot's troops crossing the Portuguese mountains, engraving after M. Orange, Bibliothèque Thiers.

91c Goya, *Ferdinand VII*, painting, Muséo del Prado.

92a Map: Spanish campaign.

92b José Casado del Alisal (1832–1886), *La réndición de Bailén*, painting, Muséo Arte Español, Madrid.

93 Louis-François Lejeune (1775–1848), *Deuxième siège de Saragosse, 8 février 1809*, painting, Versailles.

94–95 G. P. Bagetti, *Siège de Madrid*, painting, idem.

96b Fernand Cormon, *Bataille d'Essling*, painting, Musée des Beaux-Arts, Mulhouse, France.

96–97a Thevenin, *Attaque et prise de Ratisbonne* (detail), painting, Versailles.

97b Vernet, *Napoléon à Wagram*, painting, idem.

98a A. Adam, French wounded evacuated at Wagram, drawing, Grafik Sammlung, Munich.

98b Adam, scenes from the campaign of 1809, idem.

99a Adam, French wounded evacuated at Wagram, idem.

99b Adam, French soldier amputated and evacuated, idem.

100 Idem, back cover.

101 Captain Marryal, The mortal remains of Napoléon on his bed at the camp at Austerlitz, sketch drawn fourteen hours after the death of the emperor upon the request of the governor of Saint Helena, engraving (published in London July 26, 1821), Bibliothèque Thiers.

102–3b Baron Regnault, *Singature du contrat de mariage de Jérôme Bonaparte et de Fédérique-Catherine de Wurtemberg, en présence de Napoléon et Joséphine*, painting, Versailles.

103a Map: The Empire in 1811.

104b John Pott (1837–1898), *Napoléon annonce à Joséphine sa décision de divorcer*, painting, private collection.

104–5a Zix, marriage cortege of Napoléon and Marie-Louise through a gallery at the Louvre, bistre wash, Musée du Louvre.

105b Basset, birth of the king of Rome, engraving, Bibliothèque Thiers.

106 *Ambassade ottomane reçue par l'Empereur le 28 mai 1807*, watercolor, Hénnin collection, BNF.

107a Baron Gérard, *Alexandre Ier*, painting, Malmaison and Bois-Préau.

107b Napoléon reinstates the Constitution of the grand duchy of Warsaw, July 22, 1807, in Dresden, Muzeum Narodowe, Warsaw.

108–9 Louis-François Lejeune, *Bataille de la Moskowa*, painting, Versailles.

109a The burning of Moscow, 1812, Bibliothèque Marmatton.

109b Adam, wounded French soldier carried by two others, colored drawing, idem.

110–11a January Suchodoski (1797–1875), *Passage de la Bérézina*, painting, National-museum, Posen.

110b *Campagne de Moscou*, painting after Cogniet, Musée de Napoléonien, île de Aix.

111bl Faber du Faur, *Napoléon près de Pnewa, novembre 1812*, painting, Musée de l'Emperi.

111br du Faur, retreat from Moscow, December 1812, painting, idem.

112–13 A. Northern (1828–1876), *Retraite de Russie*, painting.

114 Defeat of General Vandamme at Kulm, August 30, 1813, German engraving, Bibliothèque Thiers.

115a Battle of Leipzig, German engraving, Bibliothèque Thiers.

115b Battle of Vitoria, German engraving, BNF.

116 French campaign, engraving after A. Bligny, Bibliothèque Thiers.

116–17b Idem, page 6.

118a and c Extracts of Napoléon's Act of Abdication, April 6, 1814, from *Le Moniteur*, Vinck collection, BNF.

118b Antoine Montfort (1802–1884), *Farewell to the Imperial Guard at Fontainebleau, April 20, 1814*, painting after Horace Vernet, Versailles.

118–19a Villa Napoléone of the Isle of Elba, color engraving, Bibliothèque Thiers.

119b Anonymous, *Débarquement de Napoléon à Antibes le 1er mars 1815*, gouache, Historisches Museum, Vienna.

120–21a Denis Dighton, *Attack on the British Squares by French Cavalry, Battle of Waterloo, 1815*, watercolor, National Army Museum, London.

120b Congress of Vienna (1814–15), color engraving after a painting by Jean-Baptiste Isabey.

121b Waterloo, defense of the Château d'Hougoumont by the English, idem.

122–23 Idem, page 8.

124–25a Louis Marchand, view of Longwood, Malmaison and Bois-Préau.

124b Jean-Baptiste Mauzaisse, *Napoléon sur son lit de mort*, painting, idem.

125b C. von Steuben, *Napoléon à Sainte-Hélène dictant ses mémoires au général Gourgaud*, painting, private collection.

126c Jean-Baptiste Isabey, *Embarquement du cercueil de Napoléon à bord* La Belle Poule *en rade de Jamestown*, painting, Versailles.

126–27a Codicil of Napoléon's will.

126–27b H. F. E. Philip-poteaux, *Retours des cendres: arrivée de* La Dorade *à Courbevoie le 14 décembre 1840*, painting, Malmaison and Bois-Préau.

128 "The Myth of Napoléon," postcard puzzle.

129 Coat of arms of Napoléon I, emperor of France, king of Italy, protector of the Confederation of the Rhine, and mediator of the Swiss Confederation, BNF.

130 Louis-Léopold Boilly, Joséphine in 1793, pencil drawing, Malmaison and Bois-Préau.

131 Letter from Napoléon to Joséphine, August 1804, Girod de l'Ain collection.

132 *Mémorial de Saint-Hélène*, original edition, private collection.

133 C. von Steuben, Bertrand crying beside Napoléon's corpse, lead pencil, Malmaison and Bois-Préau.

134 Napoléon decorating a grognard, engraving.

140 Isabey, *L'Apothéose de Napoléon*, watercolored lithograph after Horace Vernet, Muséo Glauco Lombardi, Parma.

142 Vivandière of the Grande Armée, engraving, BNF.

143l Louis Huart, sketch for Balzac's *La Comédie Humaine*, c. 1910, Musée Carnavalet.

143r Stendhal's handwritten title for his *Vie de Napoléon*, Musée Stendhal.

144 Baptism of the king of Rome, engraving.

146 Abel Gance, still from the film *Napoléon*, Cinémathèque de France.

148 Raffet, Bonaparte in Egypt, drawing.

149 M. A. Thiers, *Histoire de l'Empire*, 1865.

Index

A-B

Abensberg 96.

Aboukir 30, 31.

Alexander I 75, 81, *81*, 106, 107, *107*.

Alexandria 29, 30.

Amnesty for émigrés 9, *42*, 43.

Arcis-sur-Aube 117.

Arcole 20, *20*, 23.

Army of Egypt 30, *30*, 31;

- of the Alps *27*;

- of the Twenty Nations 108, 111.

Artois, count d' *39*.

Ashes, return of *126*.

Assassination attempt on Rue Saint-Nicaise *40*, 41.

Augerau *21*, 27, *86*.

Austerlitz 71, 75, *76*, 79, *85*, *99*.

Austria 20, *23*, 38, *54*, 56, 74, 75, *95*, 96, 97, *97*, 103, *106*, 107, 114, 115.

Austrian army *38*, 39, 75, *75*.

Austro-Russian forces *79*.

Bailén 92, *92*, 95, 96.

Banque de France 61.

Barras 18, 19, 27.

Bautzen 114.

Bavière 75, 96, 102.

Bayonne 91.

Beauharnais, Alexandre de *19*;

- Eugène de 19, 102, 108;

- Hortense de *19*;

- Joséphine de 19.

Bellerophon 123.

Berezina *110*, 111, *113*.

Berg, duchy of 102.

Berlin, Decree of 73, *90*;

- occupation of 80, *83*.

Bernadotte 41, *86*, 107, 115.

Berthier *21*, *86*, *108*.

Bertrand 125.

Bigot de Préameneu 64.

Blücher 120, *121*.

Bonaparte, Caroline *15*, 46;

- Charles *see* Buonaparte, Carlo;

- Elisa *15*, 102;

- Jérôme *15*, 102;

- Joseph 14, *15*, 91, *95*, 102, *114*, 117;

- Louis *15*, 102;
- Louis-Napoléon 102;
- Lucien *15*, 35, 37, 42, *102*;
- Pauline *15*, 46.
Borodino, *see* Moskowa.
Boulogne 74, *75.*
Bourbons 39, 117.
Brienne 14, *14.*
Brumaire, 18th of, 33, 34, *34*, 35, 38, 40, 42, 54, 57, 60.
Brune *36*, *86.*
Buonaparte, Carlo 14, *15*

C

Cadiz 92, *92.*
Cadoudal *46*, 47.
Cairo 29, 31.
Cambacérès 36, *36*, 40, *49*, 64, *65.*
Campaign of 1805 *75*, 77.
Campaign of 1806–7 77, 80.
Campaigns, *see specific campaign.*
Campoformio *20*, 26.
Canada 72.
Cannes 119, *119.*
Carlos IV of Spain 90, 91, *91.*
Carrousel, Arc de Triomphe du *63.*
Castiglione 20.
Caulaincourt *108.*
Champaubert 116.
Charles, archduke of Austria 96, 97, *97.*
Chateaubriand 125.
Châtelet, column at *63.*
Chaumont 117.
Chouans 41, *41.*
Civil Code 43, *53*, 64, 65, *65.*
Clary, Désirée 18.
Codes, *see specific code.*
Commercial Code 65.
Concordat 43, 57, 58, *58*, 59, *59.*
Confederation of the Rhine 80, 102.
Constitution of Year VIII (December 13, 1799) 36.
Continental System *72*, 73, *90*, 106.
Coronation 48, *48*, 49, 72.
Corsica 13, 14, *15*, 15, 16.
Council of Five Hundred 34, *35.*
Council of State 36, 37, 43, 48, 64.
Craonne 116, 117.

D-E-F

David, Jacques-Louis *39*, *48.*
Davout *80*, *86.*
Denmark 102.
Dennewitz *114.*
Desaix 30, 39.
Directory 18, 21, 26, 27, *27*, 28, 31, 33, 35, 36, 73.
Dresden 115.
Ducos 35, 36, *36.*
Dupont, General 92, *92.*
Eblé, General *110.*
Egypt, Institute of 30, *30*;
- return from 33, *33.*
Egyptian campaign 28, *28*, 29.
Elba, island of 119, *119.*
Emperor, of Austria 79, *105*;
- of Russia *79.*
Enghien, duke of *46*, 47, *47*, 72.
England 28, 38, *54*, 56, 72, *72*, 73, *73*, 74, 81, 91, *95*, 97, *103*, 103, 114, 121, *123*, 126, *126.*
Erfurt 92
Essling *86*, *96.*
Europe *71*, 75, 102.
Eylau 81, *85*, *87*, 99.
Ferdinand VII of Spain 90, 91, *91.*
Fontainebleau 117, 119, *119.*
Fouché 36, 40, *40*, 41, 42, 46, 48, 66, 68, *69*, 120.
Frankfurt conference 116.
Frederick William, king of Prussia 80.
French campaign 116, 117, *117*, 120.
Friedland 71, 81, *81*, *85.*

G-H-I-J

George III *73*, 74.
German campaign 114.
Germany *75*, *81*, 103, 104, 114, *114.*
Gourgaud 125, *125.*
Grande Armée 71, 75, *75*, 79, 80, *85*, *108*, 109, *110*, 111, *113.*
Great Empire *102*, 103.
Great Saint Bernard Pass 38, 39, *39.*
Grouchy *121.*
Helvetic Confederation 54, 102.

Hohenlinden 39.
Holland 102, 104.
Hundred Days 120.
India, loss of 72.
Institut de France 61, *61.*
Italy 39;
- Kingdom of 102.
- northern 56.
Italian campaign, first 20, *20*, 21, 26, *26*, 27, *27.*
Italian campaign, second 39.
Jacobins 40, *40*, 41.
Jena (Iéna) 71, 80, *80*, 85.
Joséphine *43*, *45*, 46, 48, *48*, 104, *104.*
Jourdan *86.*
Junot *95.*

K-L-M

Kutusov *79*, 109, *113.*
La Fère regiment 15.
Lannes *21*, 39, 86.
La Rothière 116.
Larrey, Baron *99.*
Las Cases, Emmanuel de 125, *127.*
Lassalle *21.*
Law of Pluviôse Year VIII (February 1800) 61.
Lebrun 36, *36.*
Leclerc 46.
Legion of Honor 43, *53*, *63*, 65.
Legislative Body 37, 43, 58, *63.*
Leipzig *85*, *99*, 115, *115.*
Lejeune, Edouard *108.*
Ligny 120, *121.*
Lille, count of 39, 40.
Lisbon *90.*
Lodi 20.
Lombardy *24.*
Longwood estate 124, *124.*
Louis XVIII *69*, 118, 119, 120, *120*, 126.
Louis-Philippe *126.*
Louvre, Musée du *63.*
Lowe, Hudson 125.
Lutzen 114.
MacDonald *114.*
Mack 76.
Madrid 90, 91, *91*, 92, *95.*
Malet 114.
Malmaison, Château de *43*, *45*, 47.
Malta 29, 74.
Marengo 39, 40.
Marie-Louise 105, *105*, 117.

"Marie-Louise" *117.*
Marmont 24, 117, 118.
Masséna *21*, *24*, 38, *86.*
Mayence 102.
Mémorial de Sainte-Hélène 127.
Metternich *101*, 103.
Millesimo 20.
Mombello 20, 26.
Mondovi 20.
Monge 30.
Montebello 39.
Montenotte 20.
Montereau 116.
Montholon 125.
Montmirail 116.
Moreau 39, *46.*
Moscow 108, 111, *113*;
- burning of 109, *109.*
Moskowa *85*, *99*, *108*, 109.
Murat *21*, 46, 80, *87*, 91, *91*, 102, *108*, *110*, 111, *113*, 115.

N-O-P-R

Naples 56, 115.
Nelson 30.
Ney *86*, *114*, *121.*
Niemen River 108, 111, *113.*
Nobility, imperial 66.
Oldenburg, duchy of 107.
Ottoman Empire 106.
Oudinot *114.*
Paoli, Pasquale 14, 15, 16, *16*, 17.
Peace Treaties
- of Amiens 56, *57*;
- of Florence 56;
- of Lunéville 56, *56*;
- of Paris 56;
- of Tilsit 81, *81*, *106*;
- of Vienna 97;
- with Spain 56;
- with Turkey 56;
- with the United States 56.
Penal Code 65.
Pitt, William 38, 72.
Pius VII 48, *48*, 58, 59.
Poland 81, 106.
Portalis 64.
Portugal *90*, 91.
Prague, Armistice of 115.
Prussia *80*, 103, 114.
Pyramids 29
Ramolino, Maria Letizia 14, *15.*
Rapp *79.*
Ratisbonne, *see* Regensburg.

Regensburg 96, *96*.
Revolution of 1789 16, 17, 38, 41, 49, 53, 54, *54*, 55, 57, 66, *69*, *71*, 72, 101, *103*, 113, 121, 126.
Rivoli 20, *20*.
Robespierre, Augustin 17;
- Maximilien 17, 18, *39*.
Roederer *36*, 60.
Rome 102;
- king of 105, *105*, 114.
Rural Code 65.
Russia *54*, 56, 72, 74, 103, 106, *106*, 107, 108, 114.
Russian army 38, 75, *75*, 81.
Russian campaign 69, 108.
Russian retreat *110*, 111, 113, *113*.

S-T

Saint Helena *101*, *123*, 124, 125, *126*, 127.
Saint Jean d'Acre 31.
Savary *29*, 68, *68*.
Saxony 80, 102.
Senate 37, 43, 48, *48*.
Senatus consultum of 24 Thermidor Year X 42, 43.
Sérurier 21
Sieyès 31, 35, *35*, 36, *36*.
Somsierra 92, *95*.
Soult 93, *121*.
Spain 56, 74, 90, *90*, 91, 92, 114, *114*, 115;
- war with 72, 73, 91, 91, 92, 92, 93, 95.

Sweden 80, 107, 115.
Syria 31
Talleyrand *21*, 28, 36, *37*, 40, 42, *47*, 91, 117, *120*.
Théâtre Français *69*.
Thermidor, 9th of, 18
Toulon 17, *17*, 18.
Trafalgar 76, *77*, 92.
Tribunate 37, 42, 43, 48, 58.
Tulard, Jean 57.
Turkey 56, 106, 107.
Tuscany, duchy of 102.

U-V-W-Z

United States 56, 72.
Vandamme *114*.
Vendémiaire, 13th of, *18*, 19.

Vienna 92;
- Congress of 120, *120*.
Vilna 108.
Vitebsk 109.
Vitoria *114*, 115.
Wagram 71, *85*, 96, 97, *97*, *99*, 101.
War of 1812 *72*.
Warsaw, Grand Duchy of 106, *106*, 108.
Waterloo *45*, 54, *56*, 85, *99*, *121*, 126.
Wellington *121*.
Westphalia 102, 104.
Zaragoza 93, *93*.

Photograph Credits

AKG 1, 32, 40a, 96–97a, 110a, 119b, 120b. Archives Gallimard 143r. Arthephot/Oronoz 90–91b, 91c, 92b. Bibliothèque Marmottan 87b. Bibliothèque Thiers, photos Patrick Léger spine, 14a, 17, 26b, 36, 40–41b, 42b, 54–55a, 58a, 59, 60b, 61b, 70, 91a, 101, 105b, 114, 115a, 118–119a, 118b. Bibliothèque Nationale de France 16a, 18c, 41a, 43, 46b, 56b, 63a, 65a, 66a, 72–73, 106, 107b, 115b, 118ac, 142. Bulloz 15c. Château de Grosbois, photo Musée de l'Armée/F. Cheval 28–29b. Châteaux de Malmaison and Bois-Préau 18–19, 54, 126–27a, 126–27b, 130, 133. Cinémathèque de France 144. Collection John Hay Library of Brown University, Providence, Rhode Island 88al, 88ar, 88bl, 88br, 89. Collection de Buisson, photo Patrick Léger, 100. P. Cornier 10. Dagli Orti 35b, 37b, 56–57a, 57b, 109a, 140. DR 28, 30b, 31, 42a, 65b, 68a, 69a, 71, 76, 131,134. Gallimard Jeunesse 21a, 77, 92a, 103a. Giraudon 35a, 66a. Grafik Sammlung, Munich. Photo *Tradition Magazine* plates 98al, 98bl, 99a, 99b, 109b. J.-L. Charmet 61a. Laslett John Sotheby's Picture Library 104b. Musée de l'Armée 80-81b, 86a, 86b. Musée de l'Emperi, Salon-de-Provence 111bl, 111br. Musée de Montargis 52. Musée départmentale Pascal Paoli de Morosaglia 16b. Musée Napoléon Ie, Fontainebleau 53. Musée des châteaux de Malmaison et Bois-Préau 13. National Army Museum, London 120–21a, 121b. Photothèque des Musées de la Ville de Paris 46a, 60a, 63b, 71, 143l, 146. Private collection, photo Patrick Léger 73b, 132, 144, 147. Private collection, photo Josse 125b. RMN front cover, 2, 3, 4, 5, 6, 7, 9, 12, 14h, 15a, 15b, 20–21b, 22–23, 24–25, 27, 30, 33, 34, 36a, 38, 39, 44–45, 47, 48a, 48–49b, 49a, 50–51, 55b, 58b, 62, 64, 66–67a, 67b, 68b, 69b, 74–75a, 74–75b, 78–79, 80–81a, 82–83, 84–85, 86c, 86–87a, 93, 94–95, 96b, 97b, 102–3, 104–5a, 107a, 108–9a, 110b, 116–17b, 118b, 124b, 124–25a, 125b. Roger-Viollet 18a, 19a, 19c, 128, 146. Sotheby's Picture Library 26a, 112–13. Tate Gallery Publications, London back cover, 8, 122–23. Taillandier 68–69a.

Acknowledgments

The author and Éditions Gallimard thank Sophie Béranger; Juan-Carlos Carmigniani; Bernard Chevallier, head curator at the Musées des Malmaison et Bois-Préau; Georges Liébert; the house of Girodet-Trioson; Danuta Monachon, head curator at the Bibliothèque Thiers; Marie-Annick Monet, executrix of the Grosbois estate; the Musée de Montargis; Eric Pautrel, head of the documentation department at the Musées des Malmaison et Bois-Préau; Jean-Luc Pianelli, curator of the Bibliothèque Marmottan; Alain Pigeard; Madame Sérafini, curator at the Musée départmentale de Pascal Paoli.

Thierry Lentz has published some fifteen works on the
Consulate and the Empire, including *Le Grand Consulat*
(Fayard, 1999), *Savary, le séide de Napoléon* (Fayard, 2001),
Dictionnaires des Ministres de Napoléon (Christian, 2001),
La Nouvelle Histoire du Premier Empire (3 vols., Fayard,
2001, 2004, 2005). Laureate of the Institut de France, he is
director of the Fondation Napoléon.

For Jacques Jourquin

Translated from the French by Laurel Hirsch

For Harry N. Abrams, Inc.
Project Manager: Susan Richmond
Editor: Nancy E. Cohen
Typographic designer: Tina Thompson
Cover designer: Darilyn Carnes

Library of Congress Cataloging-in-Publication Data

Lentz, Thierry.
    [Napoléon. English]
    Napoléon : "my ambition was great" / Thierry Lentz.
        p. cm. — (Discoveries)
    Translation of: Napoléon : mon ambition était grande.
    Includes bibliographical references and index.
    ISBN 0-8109-9208-6 (pbk.)
    1. Napoleon I, Emperor of the French, 1769–1821. 2. France—History—
1789–1815. 3. Emperors—France—Biography. I. Title. II. Series: Discoveries
(New York, N.Y.)
DC203.L49513 2005
944.05'092—dc22

2004024411

Printed and bound in Italy
10 9 8 7 6 5 4 3 2 1